Key Stage Two Maths Investigations

Teacher Book for Year 5

This Teacher Book accompanies CGP's Year 5 Maths Investigations Question Book.

It's matched page-to-page with the Question Book and includes background information to help teachers introduce and teach each investigation. Detailed answers are included too!

We've also made some handy printable resources to go alongside the investigations — you can download them from this page:

www.cgpbooks.co.uk/KS2-Maths-Investigations

Or you can scan this QR code:

What CGP is all about

Our sole aim here at CGP is to produce the highest quality books — carefully written, immaculately presented and dangerously close to being funny.

Then we work our socks off to get them out to you — at the cheapest possible prices.

Contents

How To Use This Book 1

Section One — Calculations

See-Saw Calculations 3
Generating number sentences involving equals, less than and greater than symbols.
- *Prerequisite learning: use of the '<' and '>' symbols, addition and subtraction with negative numbers.*

Take Four Numbers 6
Generating calculations by changing the order of a set of four digits and varying the position of the multiplication sign (or signs), and coming up with minimum and maximum products.
- *Prerequisite learning: multiplication of 3-digit numbers by 1-digit numbers, and 2-digit numbers by 2-digit numbers.*

Tests of Divisibility for 3, 6 and 9 10
Adding the digits of multiples of 3, 6 and 9, using the totals to create rules to be tested.
- *Prerequisite learning: confidence with the 3, 6 and 9 times tables.*

Factor Chains 15
Listing the factors of numbers and adding most of them to find the next number in a chain.
- *Prerequisite learning: knowledge of the times tables, ability to find factor pairs of numbers to 100 and recognition of prime numbers.*

Factors and Primes 19
Looking for links between a number and how many factors it has.
- *Prerequisite learning: knowledge of times tables, prime numbers and square numbers.*

Section Two — Fractions

Dancing By Fractions 22
Visualising fractions by coming up with moves for groups within a group of dancers.
- *Prerequisite learning: confidence with multiplication and division facts.*

Dominoes and Fractions 25
With the aid of dominoes, exploring equivalent fractions and recurring decimals.
- *Prerequisite learning: familiarity with unit fractions and non-unit fractions with common denominators.*
- *Online resources available: printable dominoes.*

Contents

Section Three — Measurement and Geometry

A Thousand Paces 28

Estimating the number of steps between home and school, and adapting this estimate based on further information about distance and step size.

- *Prerequisite learning: ability to round numbers to the nearest 10 and 100, and to one decimal place.*

Quadrilateral Areas 31

Creating quadrilaterals on pegboards and working out their areas.

- *Prerequisite learning: names of quadrilaterals, knowledge of how to find areas by counting squares.*
- *Online resource available: printable pegboards.*

Tessellations 33

Identifying which shapes do and do not tessellate, and exploring why.

- *Prerequisite learning: names of 2D shapes, knowledge that there are 360° in a full turn.*
- *Online resource available: printable 2D shapes.*

Triangle Transformations 37

Translating, rotating and reflecting triangles, and looking for patterns.

- *Prerequisite learning: names of types of triangles, ability to measure angles.*

Section Four — Statistics

Pulse Rate Line Graphs 41

Recording pulse rate after exercise and displaying the data on line graphs with different axes, to explore the effect this has on how the information appears.

- *Prerequisite learning: ability to read and draw line graphs.*

Published by CGP

ISBN: 978 1 78908 901 1

Written by Amanda MacNaughton and Mike Ollerton.

Editors: Ellen Burton, Sharon Keeley-Holden, Chris Lindle, Sam Norman
Reviewer: Clare Selway
With thanks to Caley Simpson for the proofreading.

Printed by Elanders Ltd, Newcastle upon Tyne.
Clipart from Corel®
Based on the classic CGP style created by Richard Parsons.

Text, design, layout and original illustrations © Coordination Group Publications Ltd. (CGP) 2022
All rights reserved.

Photocopying more than 5% of this book is not permitted, even if you have a CLA licence.
Extra copies are available from CGP with next day delivery • 0800 1712 712 • www.cgpbooks.co.uk

How To Use This Book

This book guides teachers through each of the investigations in the pupil book. Each page in the pupil book has an accompanying page in the teacher book, as shown below:

- The pupil page, with the answers written on in red.
- Introduction to the investigation, and list of its aims.
- List of key vocabulary, and list of required resources (if any).
- Green boxes explain extra support that can be given to struggling pupils.
- Notes with extra guidance, information and suggestions to help teaching.
- Box pointing at specific parts of the investigation that involve working at Greater Depth.
- Purple boxes suggest challenges to extend the investigation.

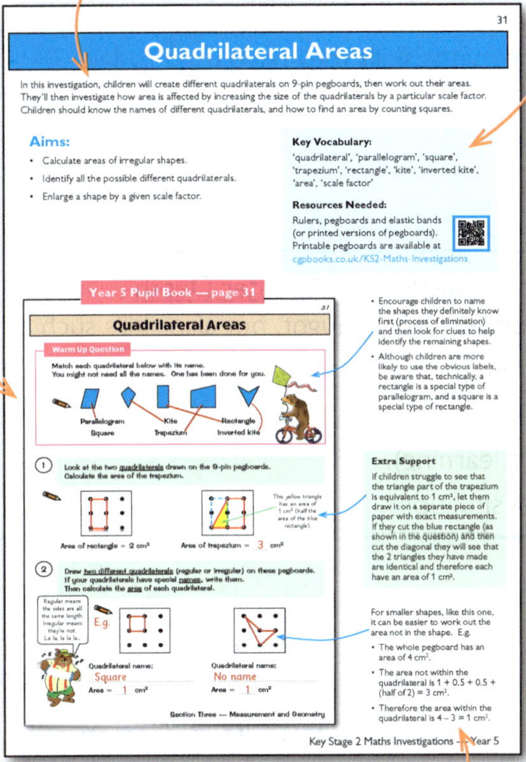

It is a good idea to read through the investigation and teacher notes before delivering each lesson, as this will allow you to prepare, e.g.:

- Required <u>resources</u> — e.g. maths manipulatives or print-outs (some investigations have accompanying printable online resources — these are found at cgpbooks.co.uk/KS2-Maths-Investigations or by scanning the QR code).

- Any other set-up — e.g. some investigations may require children to work in mixed-ability <u>pairings</u> or <u>groups</u>, and some may benefit from a large <u>space</u> being available.

- <u>Timings</u> — investigations could take varying lengths of time, depending on the learners and environment you are working in. You might need to be prepared with the suggested extra challenges, if you expect some children to finish early.

The next page gives more general advice for leading these investigations.

Key Stage 2 Maths Investigations — Year 5

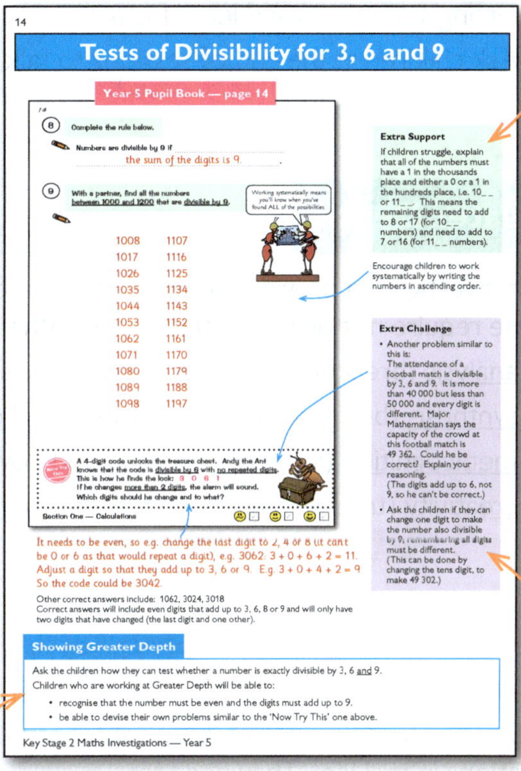

How To Use This Book

During the Lesson

- There will be many opportunities throughout these investigations to stop the lesson for a mini-plenary or quick class discussion.
- Ask the children what they have found out so far or what they have noticed.
- Ask children to demonstrate how they are being systematic.
- Regularly remind children that good mathematicians test ideas and predictions; they get things wrong sometimes and learn from it.
- Ask children at the end of sessions to talk about the maths skills they have used today.

Greater Depth

Each investigation provides opportunities for children to demonstrate 'Greater Depth'.
These require not only mastery of the mathematical concept being taught, but also skills such as:

- analysis (breaking down a problem into its component parts).
- synthesis (bringing different mathematical concepts together).
- metacognition (reflecting on what and how they are learning).
- creativity (transferring their understanding to a new situation).

Skills Needed for Completing Investigations

Maths investigations involve a special set of skills that help children to deal with mathematical situations in real life. They need to:

- work systematically (collect and work out information in an orderly way).
- spot patterns and make predictions (use evidence to decide what will happen next).
- generate rules (use evidence to make generalisations).
- show their thinking (write down their thoughts and findings).

Introduce pupils to these skills using pages 1-2 of the workbook.

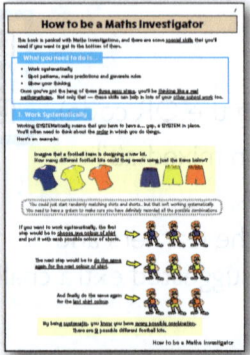 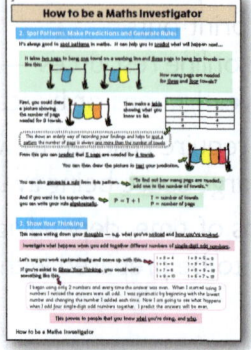

'Showing your thinking' is often called 'Journaling'. It helps children develop their reasoning skills. Thinking more deeply about the maths they are doing will help them to master mathematical concepts and show greater depth in their work.

Talk them through the examples and invite them to think of other examples of where they could apply these skills (e.g. in Science and Computer Science).

Key Stage 2 Maths Investigations — Year 5

See-Saw Calculations

Children need to understand and use the terms and symbols equals (=), less than (<) and greater than (>). Children will be generating number sentences from number cards to create positive and negative answers. They'll be expected to show order in their working and explain their thinking.

Aims:

- Create number sentences showing understanding of negative numbers.
- Count forwards and backwards with positive and negative whole numbers, including through 0.
- Work systematically to find all possibilities.
- Understand and use the terms maximum and minimum, and the symbols < and >.

Key Vocabulary:

'less than' (<), 'greater than' (>), 'maximum', 'minimum'

Resources Needed:

Scissors, card/paper (or pre-made cards)

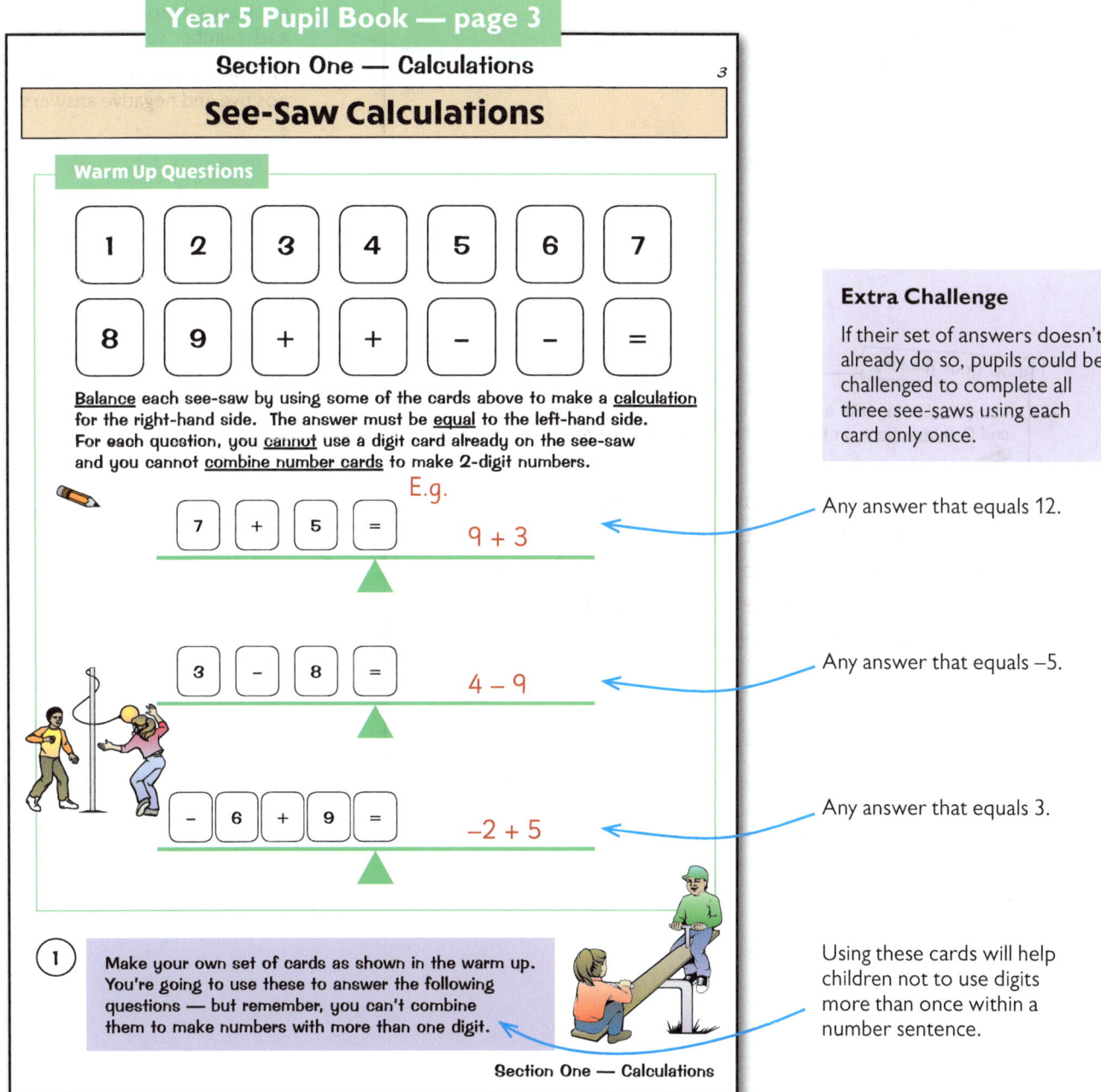

Extra Challenge

If their set of answers doesn't already do so, pupils could be challenged to complete all three see-saws using each card only once.

Any answer that equals 12.

Any answer that equals −5.

Any answer that equals 3.

Using these cards will help children not to use digits more than once within a number sentence.

Key Stage 2 Maths Investigations — Year 5

See-Saw Calculations

Year 5 Pupil Book — page 4

2 Use your cards to make <u>different balanced see-saws</u>. Some of the calculations should make <u>positive</u> numbers whilst others should make <u>negative</u> numbers. Write some of your calculations down here.

Answers will vary, e.g.
3 + 2 = 9 − 4
−5 + 1 = 3 − 7
2 + 1 = 9 − 6

- Any numbers can be used, as long as a digit is not used twice. Also, the + and − signs should not be used more than twice in each number sentence.

- Ensure children create both positive and negative answers.

Show your thinking

Is it possible to make a see-saw balanced using <u>2 additions</u> on one side and <u>2 subtractions</u> on the other side? Explain your answer.

It is not possible. You cannot get equal amounts without repeating a digit. The smallest amount possible with two additions is 6 (1 + 2 + 3), but once these digits have been used, 6 cannot be made from subtracting twice from 9, e.g. 9 − 4 − 5 = 0

Remind children of the need to back up their answer with examples.

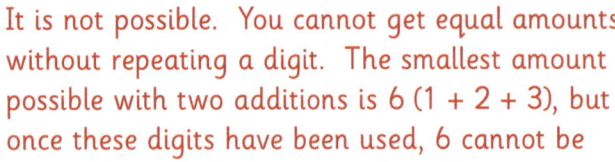

Section One — Calculations

Key Stage 2 Maths Investigations — Year 5

See-Saw Calculations

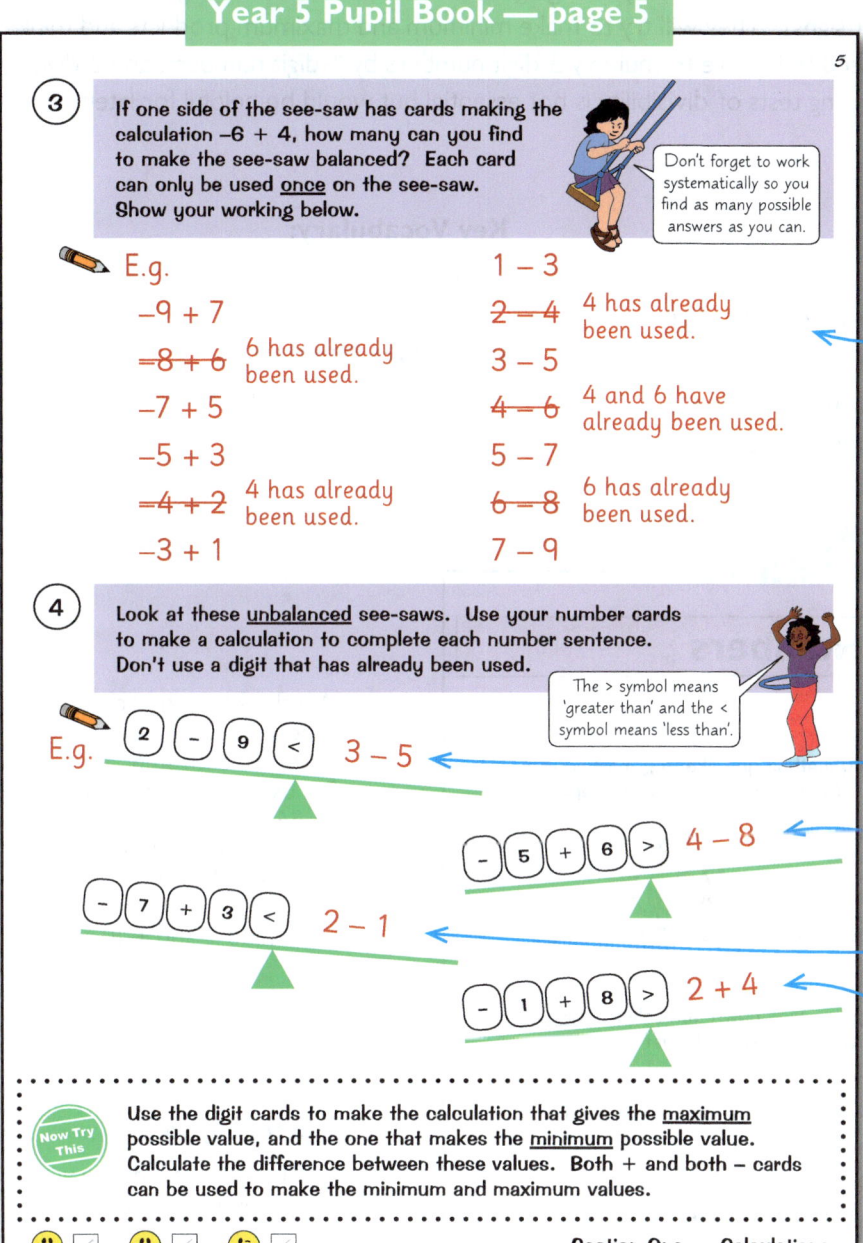

- All calculations should give the answer –2.
- These answers show systematic thinking, as they first begin with the lowest negative number possible (–9) which increases by one each time.
- The second column begins with the lowest positive number possible, and increases by one each time.
- Encourage children to write all calculations, crossing out ones they know are not allowed.
- Some children may have approached this differently and used three numbers, e.g. 1 – 5 + 2. If so, they'll have a different set of answers — as long as they all have the answer –2, they're fine.

The LHS gives –7 so the RHS needs to be greater than –7.

The LHS gives 1 so the RHS needs to be less than 1.

The LHS gives –4 so the RHS needs to be greater than –4.

The LHS gives 7 so the RHS needs to be less than 7.

For the minimum value, only two numbers are used in the calculation, because there are only two minus sign cards, and one is used to make the first number negative.

The minimum possible value is –9 – 8 = –17

The maximum possible value is 9 + 8 + 7 = 24

The difference between these two values is 41, which could be worked out using this number line:

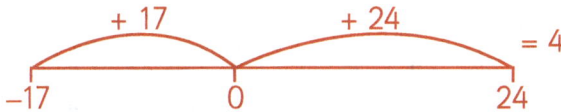

Showing Greater Depth

Children working at Greater Depth will be able to:

- (Q2 'Show Your Thinking') explain why they cannot get the two sides to be equal — they should work systematically to come up with the examples that show why it is impossible.

Key Stage 2 Maths Investigations — Year 5

Take Four Numbers

In this investigation, children will be generating calculations by changing the order of a set of four digits and varying the position of the multiplication sign (or signs). They will try to make minimum and maximum products and think about strategies for this. Children will need to be able to multiply 3-digit numbers by 1-digit numbers, and 2-digit numbers by other 2-digit numbers. Knowing tests of divisibility is not essential but would be helpful for later stages of the investigation.

Aims:
- Use multiplication facts.
- Use a chosen method to multiply 1-, 2- and 3-digit numbers.
- Look for and use strategies to create multiplications resulting in the smallest and greatest products.

Key Vocabulary:
'product'

Resources Needed:
Scrap paper, digit cards (or card to make digit cards).

Year 5 Pupil Book — page 6

Take Four Numbers

Warm Up Questions

Work out these multiplications. Use any method you like, e.g. partitioning, the grid method or short multiplication. Do any working on scrap paper.

3 × 6 = 18   3 × 6 × 2 = 36

3 × 6 × 2 × 5 = 180

362 × 5 = 1810   235 × 6 = 1410   63 × 52 = 3276

1 With a partner, place a set of digit cards face down and select four cards. Arrange all of the digits in different ways to create at least three multiplication calculations.

E.g. [3][5][6][8]   3 × 5 × 6 × 8   356 × 8   5 × 6 × 38   63 × 85

I have selected the digits: E.g. 9   1   2   5

The multiplication calculations I have created are:

E.g. 2 × 1 × 5 × 9   251 × 9
      2 × 5 × 19   52 × 19

2 Find the answer to each multiplication calculation using a method of your choice. Record each multiplication and product below.

You might need some scrap paper for your working.

E.g. 2 × 1 × 5 × 9 = 90   251 × 9 = 2259
      2 × 5 × 19 = 190   52 × 19 = 988

The 'product' of a set of numbers is what you get when you multiply them together.

Section One — Calculations

Whichever method children choose to use, encourage them to record each step.
E.g. using the partition method, for 362 × 5:
  300 × 5 = 1500,
  60 × 5 = 300,
  2 × 5 = 10,
  1500 + 300 + 10 = 1810.

Extra Support
- If children need help with generating calculations, suggest that they use some of the example calculations above as a template, i.e. the four digits multiplied individually, a 3-digit number multiplied by a 1-digit number, 2 single digits multiplied then multiplied by a 2-digit number, and finally two 2-digit numbers multiplied together. To generate more, they can use the same pattern but change the order of the digits.
- You could give children a certain number of calculations to aim for, depending on their ability.

Key Stage 2 Maths Investigations — Year 5

Take Four Numbers

Year 5 Pupil Book — page 7

③ Which of your multiplications gave the greatest and smallest products?

Greatest product: E.g.   251 × 9 = 2259
Smallest product: 2 × 1 × 5 × 9 = 90

④ Work with your partner to try to find a calculation which gives an even greater product. Record the calculations you try and their products below.

E.g.   921 × 5 = 4605
521 × 9 = 4689
95 × 21 = 1995
51 × 92 = 4692
52 × 91 = 4732

So the calculation that gives the greatest product is: 52 × 91

Show your thinking

Explain how you arranged the digits to give the greatest value.

The largest digits were put in the tens columns of the 2-digit numbers.
52 × 91 gives a higher value than 51 × 92 because 2 × 91 + 1 × 52 is bigger than 2 × 51 + 1 × 92.

Section One — Calculations

- Working in pairs means children can compare their answers to ensure they are correct. Tell children that if they have different answers, they will need to check their own or each other's methods.

- The smallest product will be created from the four individual digits being multiplied together, i.e. 2 × 1 × 5 × 9.

- The greatest product will be created by two 2-digit numbers being multiplied together. The digits must be arranged so that the larger digits are in the tens places, e.g. 52 × 19 = 988 but 52 × 91 = 4732. The smallest digit must then be put in the ones place next to the largest digit.

Extra Support

If children only try 3-digit numbers multiplied by 1-digit numbers, suggest that they could try multiplying two 2-digit numbers together.

Extra Challenge

Children who are working quickly could, at this point, consider:

- What would happen if 5 or 6 cards were used?
- Would the patterns and results be the same?
- Can you explain it?

The grid method of multiplication is a good way to show why placing the largest digits in the tens columns gives the greatest product.

E.g.

×	50	2
90	4500	180
1	50	2

compared with

×	20	5
10	200	50
9	180	45

The grid method can also show why multiplying a 3-digit number by a 1-digit number won't give as large a product.

E.g.

×	900	20	1
5	4500	100	5

Key Stage 2 Maths Investigations — Year 5

Take Four Numbers

It would be useful for children to see the calculations which produced the greatest and smallest products for other pairs of children at this stage. They could either join together with another pair and discuss their findings, or the class could be drawn together in a mini-plenary.

Year 5 Pupil Book — page 8

5) Shuffle the digit cards, place them face down and select <u>four new cards</u>. Using <u>all four digits</u>, create different <u>multiplication calculations</u> with the aim of finding the <u>smallest</u> and the <u>greatest</u> possible products.

I have selected the digits: E.g. 3   4   8   6

3 × 4 × 8 × 6 = 576
843 × 6 = 5058
643 × 8 = 5144
83 × 64 = 5312
63 × 84 = 5292

The smallest possible product is   576   .
The greatest possible product is   5312   .

Show your thinking

Explain the <u>strategies</u> you used to find the multiplications which give the smallest and greatest products.

To find the smallest product we multiplied all the single digits together.

To find the biggest product we multiplied two 2-digit numbers together. We put the biggest two digits in the tens places and put the smallest digit in the ones place next to the biggest digit.

Section One — Calculations

Children should not need to create lots of different calculations if they have understood how the smallest and greatest values are reached.

Children should understand the commutativity law of multiplication, i.e. it doesn't matter which way round the numbers are multiplied.

Some children might not see the relationship between the positions of the smaller two digits and size of the product and may simply test the smaller digits in each place to find the greatest product.

Take Four Numbers

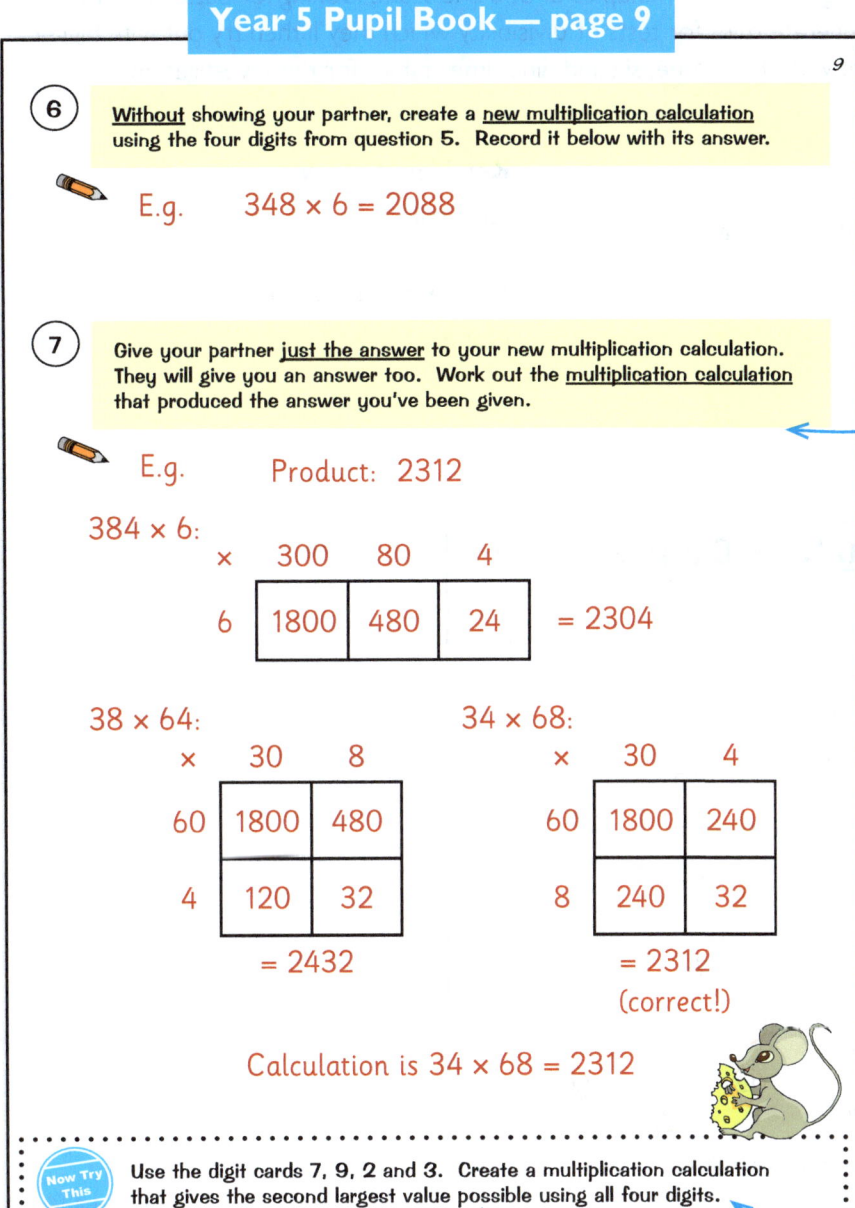

There are 37 possible multiplication calculations using 4 digits, so children will find it useful to use approximation to identify calculations that are worth trying out. For example:

- $6 \times 800 = 4800$,
  $600 \times 8 = 4800$,
  $60 \times 80 = 4800$,
  $400 \times 8 = 3200$,
  $800 \times 4 = 3200$,
  $80 \times 40 = 3200$,
  $600 \times 4 = 2400$,
  $400 \times 6 = 2400$,
  $60 \times 40 = 2400$,
  $300 \times 8 = 2400$,
  $30 \times 80 = 2400$ and
  $800 \times 3 = 2400$, so calculations that involve these digits in these positions will result in a product that is too large.

- $6 \times 300 = 1800$,
  $600 \times 3 = 1800$ and
  $60 \times 30 = 1800$
  so calculations that involve these digits in these positions are worth trying.

- $4 \times 300 = 1200$,
  $3 \times 400 = 1200$ and
  $40 \times 30 = 1200$.
  1200 is a lot smaller than 2312, so calculations that involve these digits in these positions are likely to give a product that is too low.

If children are struggling, their partner could give them a hint such as 'it's a 1-digit number multiplied by a 3-digit number' or 'I used two 2-digit numbers'.

Extra Challenge
More able pupils could push this activity further by adding in more cards.

The largest value is formed by putting the largest two digits in the tens places, then pairing the smallest digit with the largest digit, i.e. 92×73 $(= 6716)$ so the second largest product needs the same digits in the tens column but the ones digits swapped, i.e. 93×72 $(= 6696)$.

Showing Greater Depth

Children working at Greater Depth will be able to:

- (Q4-5) identify in which positions the smaller two digits should go to produce the highest product, and explain the reason for this.
- (Q7) use approximation to decide which calculations are worth trying and which can be eliminated.
- (Now Try This) apply what they discovered earlier in the investigation in order to arrange the digits to produce the second largest product, without needing to try out different variations.

Key Stage 2 Maths Investigations — Year 5

Tests of Divisibility for 3, 6 and 9

In this investigation, children will be adding the digits of multiples of 3, 6 and 9 and looking for patterns in the totals. These patterns will be used to generate rules for tests of divisibility which they'll then try out with bigger numbers. Children need to be confident with their three, six and nine times tables for this investigation.

Aims:

- Know division facts for the 3, 6 and 9 times tables.
- Look for patterns to generate rules.
- Test rules of divisibility.

Key Vocabulary:
'divisibility'

Resources Needed:
None.

Year 5 Pupil Book — page 10

Tests of Divisibility for 3, 6 and 9

Warm Up Questions

Work out these divisions.

If you know your times tables, these should be easy peasy.

27 ÷ 3 = 9   42 ÷ 6 = 7   24 ÷ 6 = 4
18 ÷ 9 = 2   36 ÷ 3 = 12   72 ÷ 9 = 8
54 ÷ 6 = 9   81 ÷ 9 = 9   21 ÷ 3 = 7
108 ÷ 9 = 12   24 ÷ 3 = 8   36 ÷ 6 = 6

1 Circle the numbers below that appear in the <u>3 times table</u>.

25   (15)   (18)   29
(33)   (21)   32   20   (24)
14   (12)
(27)   22   (36)

Now <u>add the digits</u> of each of the numbers you have circled.
E.g. 36: 3 + 6 = 9

33: 3 + 3 = 6   18: 1 + 8 = 9
21: 2 + 1 = 3   12: 1 + 2 = 3
27: 2 + 7 = 9   24: 2 + 4 = 6
15: 1 + 5 = 6

What do you notice about the <u>sums of the digits</u>?
They are all 3, 6 or 9.

Section One — Calculations

If there's time, ask the children to write all of the numbers from the 3 times table in order of size. They will notice that the pattern in the sum of the digits is repeated: 3, 6, 9, 3, 6, 9, 3, 6, 9…

Children might say that the sums of the digits are all in the 3 times table, or that they are multiples of 3. While these things are correct, children should also note that the sums of the digits are the first three multiples of three only — but this only works up to 3 × 12.

Key Stage 2 Maths Investigations — Year 5

Tests of Divisibility for 3, 6 and 9

Year 5 Pupil Book — page 11

2 The numbers in the 3 times table are <u>divisible by 3</u>. You can apply what you noticed in question 1 to <u>any number</u> to find out if it is divisible by 3.

E.g. 372: 3 + 7 + 2 = 12. This is still a 2-digit number, so add the digits again...
1 + 2 = 3 so 372 is divisible by 3.

Now try 7434. Is it divisible by 3?

7 + 4 + 3 + 4 = 18,   1 + 8 = 9
So 7434 is divisible by 3.

Keep adding the digits until you get a 1-digit number.

Emphasise the importance of repeating the process until a single digit is found.

3 Work with a partner. Give each other some 3-, 4- or 5-digit numbers to test for divisibility by 3. Show your working below. <u>Tick</u> the numbers that <u>are</u> divisible by 3 and <u>cross</u> the ones that <u>aren't</u>.

E.g. 931:   9 + 3 + 1 = 13,   1 + 3 = 4 ✗
452:   4 + 5 + 2 = 11,   1 + 1 = 2 ✗
6231:   6 + 2 + 3 + 1 = 12,   1 + 2 = 3 ✓
4520:   4 + 5 + 2 + 0 = 11,   1 + 1 = 2 ✗
10 323:   1 + 0 + 3 + 2 + 3 = 9 ✓
61 439:   6 + 1 + 4 + 3 + 9 = 23,   2 + 3 = 5 ✗

It is important the children show their working. This means that they can check each other's work in pairs and they are more likely to remember the process for another time.

Show your thinking

Can you tell if a number is divisible by 3 from whether it is odd or even? Prove it!

No, because there are both odd and even numbers that are divisible by 3. E.g.
Odd: 9 ÷ 3 = 3
Even: 6 ÷ 3 = 2

Section One — Calculations

This question will prepare pupils for the next part of the investigation. Children may notice that multiples of 3 alternate between odd and even.

Key Stage 2 Maths Investigations — Year 5

Tests of Divisibility for 3, 6 and 9

Year 5 Pupil Book — page 12

④ Circle the numbers below that appear in the <u>6 times tables</u>.

(24)   16   (18)
38   56   (42)   (30)
(60)   (72)   (54)
(48)   (66)   52   64

Now <u>add the digits</u> of each of the numbers you have circled.
E.g. 66: 6 + 6 = 12, 1 + 2 = 3

48: 4 + 8 = 12, 1 + 2 = 3
24: 2 + 4 = 6
60: 6 + 0 = 6
72: 7 + 2 = 9
42: 4 + 2 = 6
18: 1 + 8 = 9
54: 5 + 4 = 9
30: 3 + 0 = 3

What do you notice about the <u>sums of the digits</u>?
They are all 3, 6 or 9.

⑤ Think about these questions:
• What do you notice about the numbers in the 6 times table?
• Is this similar to or different from the numbers in the 3 times table?
Use these ideas to help you complete the rule below.

Numbers are divisible by 6 if they are both ___even___ and when you add their digits, they make _3_ , _6_ or _9_ .

Section One — Calculations

Extra Support

If children struggle to remember their 6 times table, remind them that each of the answers is double the 3 times table, e.g. to work out if 42 is in the 6 times table, halve it, and see if the number you get is in the 3 times table, i.e. 42 ÷ 2 = 21, which is 3 x 7, therefore 42 is in the 6 times table.

When the sum of the digits is calculated, it always makes 3, 6 or 9 (the same as the 3 times table answers).

Extra Challenge

Following on from the extra challenge from question 1, children could write all of the numbers from the 6 times table in order, and compare the pattern in the sums with that of the 3 times table. They will notice that it is 6, 3, 9, 6, 3, 9... this time.

They should notice that all of the numbers in the 6 times table are even. This feature distinguishes numbers divisible by 6 from those divisible by 3.

Key Stage 2 Maths Investigations — Year 5

Tests of Divisibility for 3, 6 and 9

Year 5 Pupil Book — page 13

⑥ With a partner, use this rule to create a list of at least three 3-digit numbers, three 4-digit numbers and three 5-digit numbers that are all divisible by 6.

E.g. 3 digits	4 digits	5 digits	Sum of the digits
132	1122	11 112	6
612	4212	22 212	9
342	3222	12 222	9
300	1200	11 100	3
912	4512	42 312	12, 1 + 2 = 3

⑦ Circle the numbers below that appear in the 9 times table.

29   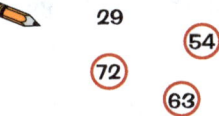   38
    40
      84   108
63   75   45

Now add the digits of each of the numbers you have circled e.g. 72: 7 + 2 = 9

54: 5 + 4 = 9   36: 3 + 6 = 9
63: 6 + 3 = 9   45: 4 + 5 = 9
18: 1 + 8 = 9   81: 8 + 1 = 9
99: 9 + 9 = 18, 1 + 8 = 9   108: 1 + 0 + 8 = 9

What do you notice about the sums of the digits?

The sum of the digits is always 9.

Are numbers in the 9 times table all odd, all even, or can they be either? How does this compare to the 3 and 6 times tables?

Numbers in the 9 times table alternate between odd or even. In the 6 times table, they're always even, and in the 3 times table, they can be either.

Section One — Calculations

Working with a partner will allow children to verbalise their thinking as they choose digits to make numbers which are divisible by 6.

Extra Support

- If children are struggling, tell them to start by placing an even digit in the ones column. They then need to choose any digit for the first or second digit. For the final digit, they have to use a digit that makes the sum of the digits 3, 6 or 9. They can follow a similar process for 4- and 5-digit numbers.

- Alternatively, 4- and 5-digit numbers can be generated by partitioning a digit in one of their 3-digit numbers. E.g. 132 divides by 6, so split the 3 into 1 + 2 to give 1122, then split the 2 in the tens place to give 11 112. The resulting numbers must still be even though.

Ask the children to recap what the divisibility test for 3, 6 and 9 are:

- If a number is divisible by 3, the digits add to make 3, 6 or 9.
- If a number is divisible by 6, it is even and the digits add to make 3, 6 or 9.
- If a number is divisible by 9, the digits add to make 9.

Tests of Divisibility for 3, 6 and 9

Year 5 Pupil Book — page 14

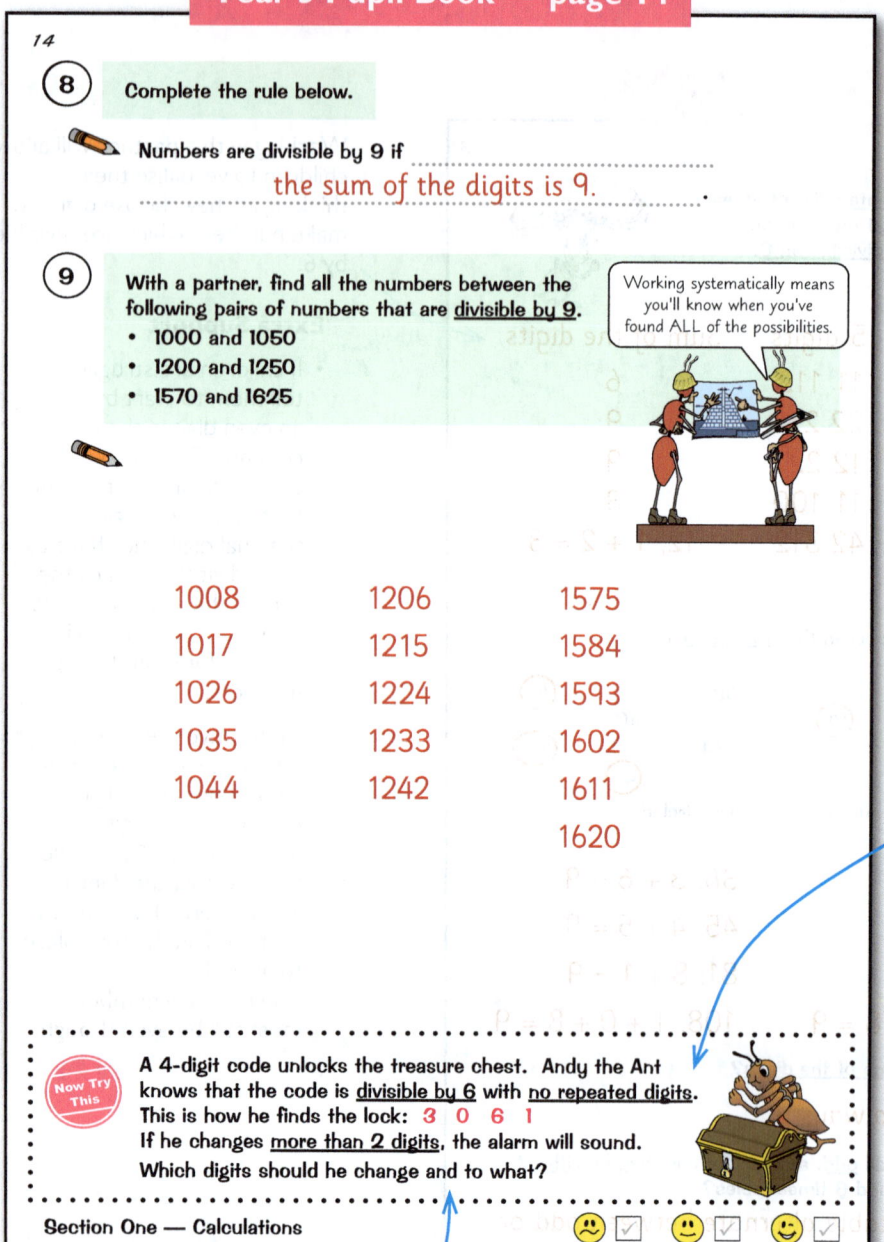

It needs to be even, so e.g. change the last digit to 2, 4 or 8 (it can't be 0 or 6 as that would repeat a digit), 3062: 3 + 0 + 6 + 2 = 11. Adjust a digit so that they add up to 3, 6 or 9. 3 + 0 + 4 + 2 = 9 So the code could be 3042.

Other correct answers include: 1062, 3024, 3018
Correct answers will be even, and have digits that add up to 3, 6 or 9. Only two digits will have been changed (the last digit and one other).

Showing Greater Depth

Children who are working at Greater Depth will be able to:
- (Now Try This) devise their own problems similar to this one.
- recognise that the number must be even and the digits must add up to 9, when asked to test whether a number is exactly divisible by 3, 6 and 9.

Factor Chains

Children will be listing the factors for given numbers and adding most of them to find the next number in a chain. They will then combine factor chains into a large interconnected diagram. For this investigation, children need to know their times tables and apply them to find factors. They should also be able to identify factor pairs of numbers to 100 and recognise prime numbers.

Aims:

- Use multiplication facts.
- List factors of numbers to 100.
- Recognise prime numbers.
- Compare lists of numbers and look for patterns.

Key Vocabulary:

'factor pair', 'prime number'

Resources Needed:

None.

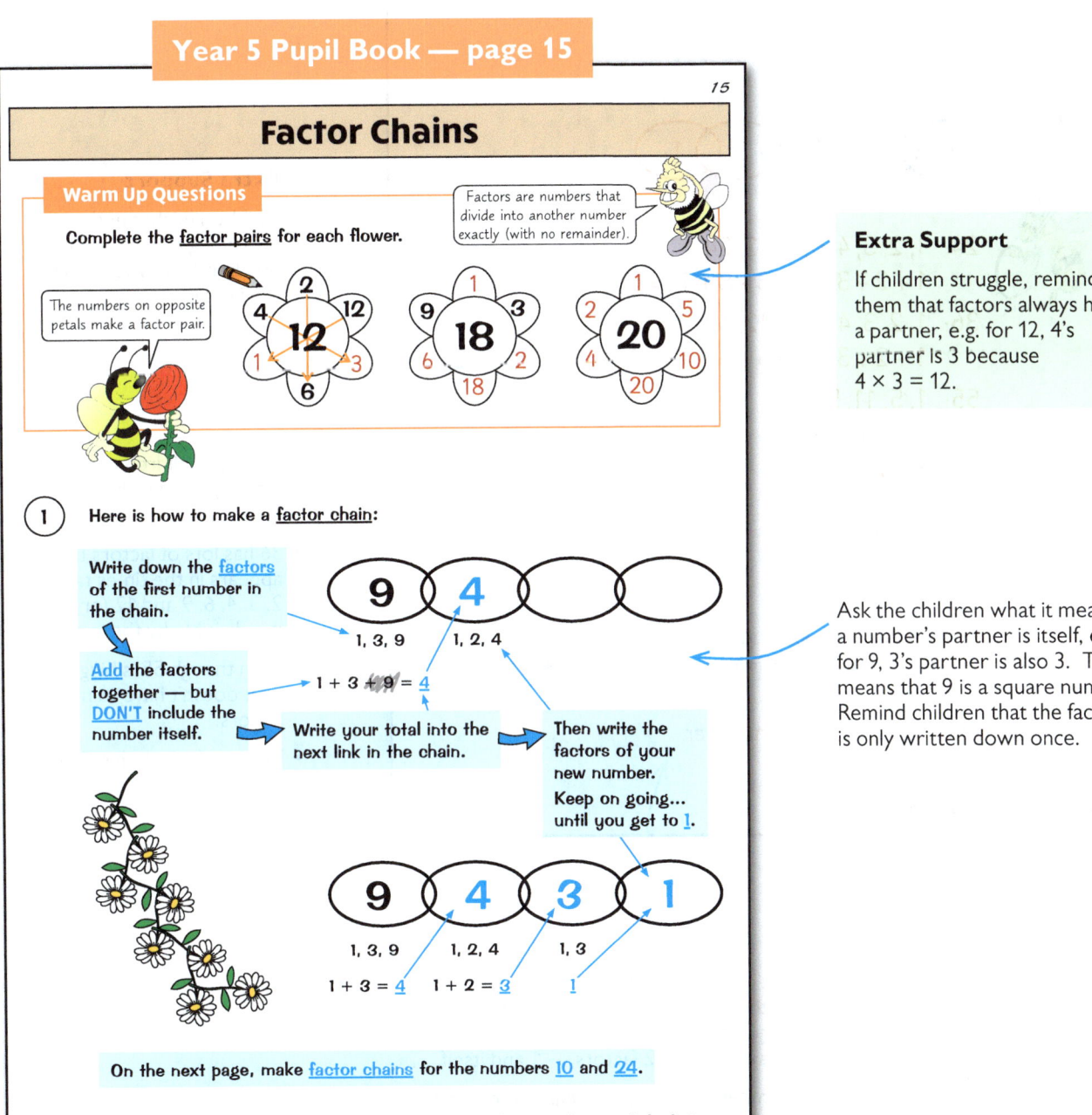

Ask the children what it means if a number's partner is itself, e.g. for 9, 3's partner is also 3. This means that 9 is a square number. Remind children that the factor 3 is only written down once.

Factor Chains

Year 5 Pupil Book — page 16

10: 1, 2, 5, 10   1 + 2 + 5 = 8
8: 1, 2, 4, 8   1 + 2 + 4 = 7
7: 1, 7   1 = 1

You might have to add some links to this chain.

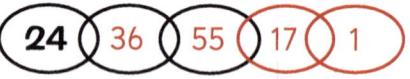

24: 1, 2, 3, 4, 6, 8, 12, 24
    1 + 2 + 3 + 4 + 6 + 8 + 12 = 36
36: 1, 2, 3, 4, 6, 9, 12, 18, 36
    1 + 2 + 3 + 4 + 6 + 9 + 12 + 18 = 55
55: 1, 5, 11, 55
    1 + 5 + 11 = 17
17 : 1, 17
     1 = 1

2 Compare the factor chains for 9, 10 and 24.
What do you notice about the number that comes just before 1?

It is always a prime number.

Section One — Calculations

Discuss with the children a good way of being systematic when finding all the factors of a number. They are best to begin with 1 (which has the number itself as its partner), then see if the number is divisible by 2 to get the next pair of factors, then by 3, then by 4 and so on until you get to a factor you have already written down as a partner.

Extra Support

Children might need reminding to exclude the number itself when adding the factors.

Encourage children to talk about what they notice when they are working, e.g.:

- 36 has lots of factors because it appears in the times tables of 2, 3, 4, 6, 9 and 12 (or because it is divisible by these numbers).
- Even though 55 is bigger than 36 it doesn't have as many factors.
- The numbers in this chain get bigger and then get smaller.

- At first some children might just notice that the number that comes before 1 is odd. If so, tell them that this is true but there is something even more interesting about it and suggest they look at its factors. They should then notice that the number always has only 2 factors — 1 and itself.
- Remind them that these numbers have a special name (or, if this is their first experience of them, tell them that they are called prime numbers).

Key Stage 2 Maths Investigations — Year 5

Factor Chains

Year 5 Pupil Book — page 17

③ Choose at least 3 more numbers and make factor chains for them. Choose numbers that are less than 30.

E.g.

8 — 7 — 1

8: 1, 2, 4, 8   1 + 2 + 4 = 7
7: 1, 7   1 = 1

16 — 15 — 9 — 4 — 3 — 1

16: 1, 2, 4, 8, 16   1 + 2 + 4 + 8 = 15
15: 1, 3, 5, 15   1 + 3 + 5 = 9
9: 1, 3, 9   1 + 3 = 4
4: 1, 2, 4   1 + 2 = 3
3: 1, 3   1 = 1

28 — 28 — ...

28: 1, 2, 4, 7, 14, 28   1 + 2 + 4 + 7 + 14 = 28

You could compare your factor chains with others that your classmates have made. Are there any similarities between them?

Show your thinking

Write down any patterns or things you notice in your factor chains.

E.g.
Factor chains can lead on into other factor chains. For example, 9 gives 9—4—3—1, and 16 gives 16—15—9—4—3—1.
Numbers in factor chains can get bigger before getting smaller.

Section One — Calculations

- All factor chains from 2 to 30 are shown on the next page of this book, which you can use to check answers for this question.

- Between 0 and 10, there are 4 prime numbers (2, 3, 5, 7) so these numbers will go directly to 1 in the second link. Encourage children not to choose prime numbers.

- The factor chain for 16 joins up with the factor chain for 9 shown on page 15.

- The number 6 leads to a never-ending factor chain, with 6 in each link. The number 28 does the same. These are known as 'perfect numbers'.

Extra Challenge

Consider introducing the concept of perfect numbers to children. Ask them if they can define a perfect number. They could fill in the blanks in this sentence:
"A perfect number is a number which is ………. to the ………. of its ………….., excluding ……………………………."
Answer: equal, sum, factors, the number itself.

- Encourage children to share and discuss their factor chains.

- Ask children to consider which numbers they would expect to have long factor chains. They may make a prediction — e.g. the higher the number, the longer the factor chain. They can test this prediction and disprove it.

- You could ask children to choose a number and make a prediction about the length of its factor chain, giving reasons, e.g. 'I predict it will have a long factor chain because it has a lot of factors.' They can then test their prediction and comment on it. Or they may make predictions about odd/even numbers. Encourage them to test their predictions.

Factor Chains

Year 5 Pupil Book — page 18

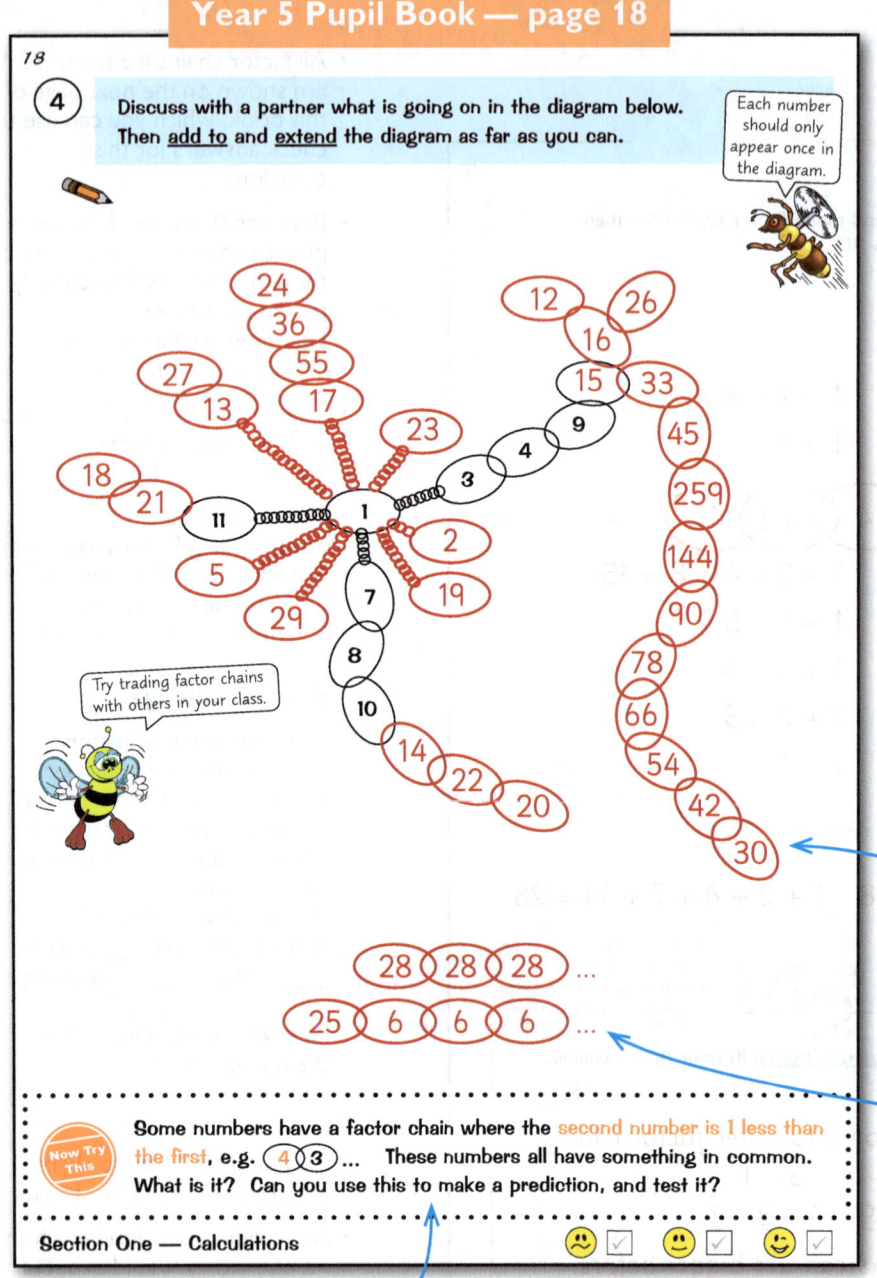

- This diagram shows the factor chains for all numbers up to 30, and how they 'link together', or feed into one another.

- You may wish to give children strips of paper and felt tips so they can present their factor chains and describe what they have noticed. Then they can combine their chains to create a physical version of this diagram, e.g. by sticking them onto a wall with sticky tack.

- Children will need a rubber handy, as they are likely to make mistakes, and to realise that they have duplicated number chains.

- Encourage pupils to check that they have included all numbers up to 20 (and then 30), and that each number only appears once. This will require children to work systematically.

- The chain beginning with 30 is very long! But it may be quite fun, as the numbers ramp up and it feels like it's going to spiral out of control... only for it to suddenly drop from 259 to 45. This one could be done as a whole class, using the internet to look up factors, and perhaps checking the additions on a calculator.

- Consider introducing the concept of perfect numbers if you haven't done so already (see previous page). These are the only numbers not to lead to 1. The next perfect number is 496.

These are the numbers 2, 4, 8, and 16. They have doubled each time. I predict that the second number in the factor chain for 32 will be 31.
32: 1 + 2 + 4 + 8 + 16 = <u>31</u>
Now I'll investigate 64: 1 + 2 + 4 + 8 + 16 + 32 = <u>63</u>

The numbers in this pattern are the powers of 2, i.e. $2^1 = 2$, $2^2 = 4$, $2^3 = 8$ etc.
(You may not want to introduce children to power notation, but you could elicit the concept: $4 = 2 \times ?$ $8 = 2 \times ? \times ?$ ...)

Showing Greater Depth

Children who are working at Greater Depth will have successfully worked through the Now Try This activity. They could then try to spot a pattern for the powers of 3 (3, 9, 27...).

- "We've looked at 2, then 2 × 2, then 2 × 2 × 2, etc. What about 3, 3 × 3, 3 × 3 × 3, etc.?"
- Children then find the second number in the factor chains. (3—<u>1</u>, 9—<u>4</u>..., 27—<u>13</u>...)
- "Is there a rule to get from the first to the second number?" (Subtract 1 then divide by 2.)
- Pupils then test their rule on the next power of 3 (81). If their rule didn't work, they can modify it.

Key Stage 2 Maths Investigations — Year 5

Factors and Primes

In this investigation, children will be looking for links between a number and how many factors it has. They'll notice that prime numbers have exactly two factors and that square numbers have an odd number of factors. They'll also shade factors on a grid and describe patterns they notice. Knowledge of times tables, and also prime and square numbers, is needed for this investigation.

Aims:

- Use multiplication facts.
- List factors of numbers to 25.
- Recognise prime and square numbers.
- Identify and describe patterns.

Key Vocabulary:

'factor', 'prime number', 'square number'

Resources Needed:

Colouring pencils.

Year 5 Pupil Book — page 19

Factors and Primes

Warm Up Question

Complete the multiplication grid (it's been started for you).
The only factors of 5 are 1 and 5.
Circle the 4s you've written (there should be 3 of them). Think about how you can tell from the table that the factors of 4 are 1, 2 and 4.

×	1	2	3	4	5	6	7	8	9	10
5	5	10	15	20	25	30	35	40	45	50
4	(4)	8	12	16	20	24	28	32	36	40
3	3	6	9	12	15	18	21	24	27	30
2	2	(4)	6	8	10	12	14	16	18	20
1	1	2	3	(4)	5	6	7	8	9	10

4 only appears in the rows and columns of 1, 2 and 4, which shows that these are its factors.

1. List the <u>factors</u> of each number below. Then count <u>how many factors</u> each has and fill in the table.

You can look at the grid above for help.

- 1: 1
- 2: 1, 2
- 3: 1, 3
- 4: 1, 2, 4
- 5: 1, 5
- 6: 1, 2, 3, 6
- 8: 1, 2, 4, 8
- 9: 1, 3, 9
- 10: 1, 2, 5, 10
- 12: 1, 2, 3, 4, 6, 12
- 15: 1, 3, 5, 15
- 16: 1, 2, 4, 8, 16
- 20: 1, 2, 4, 5, 10, 20
- 25: 1, 5, 25

Children may need reminding to include 1 and the number itself in each set of factors.

Number	1	2	3	4	5	6	8	9	10	12	15	16	20	25
Number of factors	1	2	2	3	2	4	4	3	4	6	4	5	6	3

What do you notice about the numbers that have an <u>odd number of factors</u>?
They are square numbers.

Section One — Calculations

Extra Support

If children cannot see what the numbers 1, 4, 9, 16 and 25 have in common, tell them to consider them as answers to times table questions, e.g.
_ × _ = 1   _ × _ = 4
_ × _ = 9   _ × _ = 16
_ × _ = 25

They should then notice that they are the answers when a number is multiplied by itself.

Key Stage 2 Maths Investigations — Year 5

Factors and Primes

Year 5 Pupil Book — page 20

② Write down all the numbers up to 25 that you weren't asked about in question 1. Write their factors next to them.

7: 1, 7
11: 1, 11
13: 1, 13
14: 1, 2, 7, 14
17: 1, 17
18: 1, 2, 3, 6, 9, 18
19: 1, 19
21: 1, 3, 7, 21
22: 1, 2, 11, 22
23: 1, 23
24: 1, 2, 3, 4, 6, 8, 12, 24

Count how many factors each number has and complete the table below.

Number	7	11	13	14	17	18	19	21	22	23	24
Number of factors	2	2	2	4	2	6	2	4	4	2	8

Complete the following sentences:
Numbers that have only two factors are called __prime numbers__.
Their factors are always __1__ and __themselves__.
Numbers that have more than two factors are called __composite numbers__.

Section One — Calculations

Extra Support
Children sometimes muddle up the terms factor and multiple. Remind them that multiples involve multiplying.

Children could compare their factor list with their partner's list to check it is correct.

A common misconception is to think that 1 is a prime number. This usually comes from being told that prime numbers are only divisible by themselves and 1. However, prime numbers must have exactly two factors, which of course 1 doesn't.

At Year 5, children should also know that non-prime numbers are called composite numbers, be able to recall the prime numbers up to 19, and decide if any number up to 100 is prime.

Factors and Primes

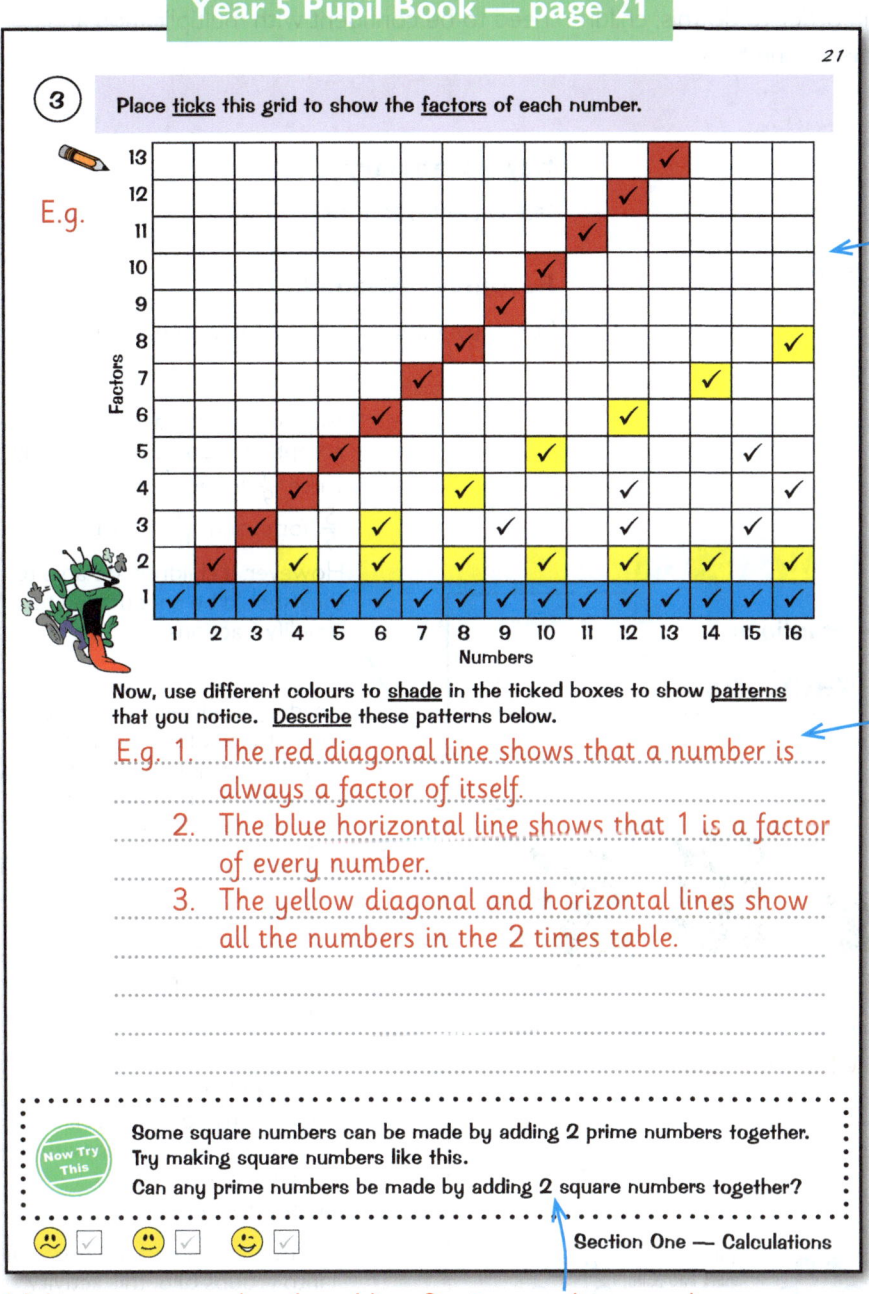

Year 5 Pupil Book — page 21

Making square numbers by adding 2 prime numbers together:
1: cannot be made, 4 = 2 + 2, 9 = 2 + 7, 16 = 5 + 11 or 3 + 13, 25 = 2 + 23, 36 = 5 + 31 or 7 + 29 or 13 + 23 or 17 + 19, 49 = 2 + 47, 64 = 3 + 61 or 5 + 59 or 11 + 53 or 17 + 47 or 23 + 41, 81 = 2 + 79, 100 = 3 + 97 or 11 + 89 or 17 + 83 or 29 + 71 or 41 + 59 or 47 + 53

Making prime numbers by adding 2 square numbers together:
1 + 4 = 5, 4 + 9 = 13, 9 + 64 = 73, 16 + 25 = 41, 25 + 36 = 61, 1 + 16 = 17, 4 + 25 = 29, 16 + 81 = 97, 25 + 64 = 89, 1 + 36 = 37, 4 + 49 = 53

Showing Greater Depth

As part of the 'Now Try This' task, ask the children if they notice any patterns in how square numbers can be made by adding two prime numbers. Children working at greater depth should be able to explain that:

- odd square numbers can only be made by adding 2 to another prime number because 2 is the only even prime number, and you need to add an even number and an odd number to get an odd total.
- the bigger the even square number, the more ways it can be made by adding two prime numbers.

Key Stage 2 Maths Investigations — Year 5

Dancing By Fractions

In this investigation, children will work in groups to visually represent fractions. They'll create simple dance moves to show fractions of whole numbers. In order to do this, children need to be confident with multiplication and division facts, and be familiar with factors of numbers.

Aims:

- Identify equivalent fractions.
- Recognise and show, using visual representations, families of common equivalent fractions.
- Connect division and multiplication to finding fractions of a number.

Key Vocabulary:
'equivalent fractions'

Resources Needed:
Space to get into groups and move around.

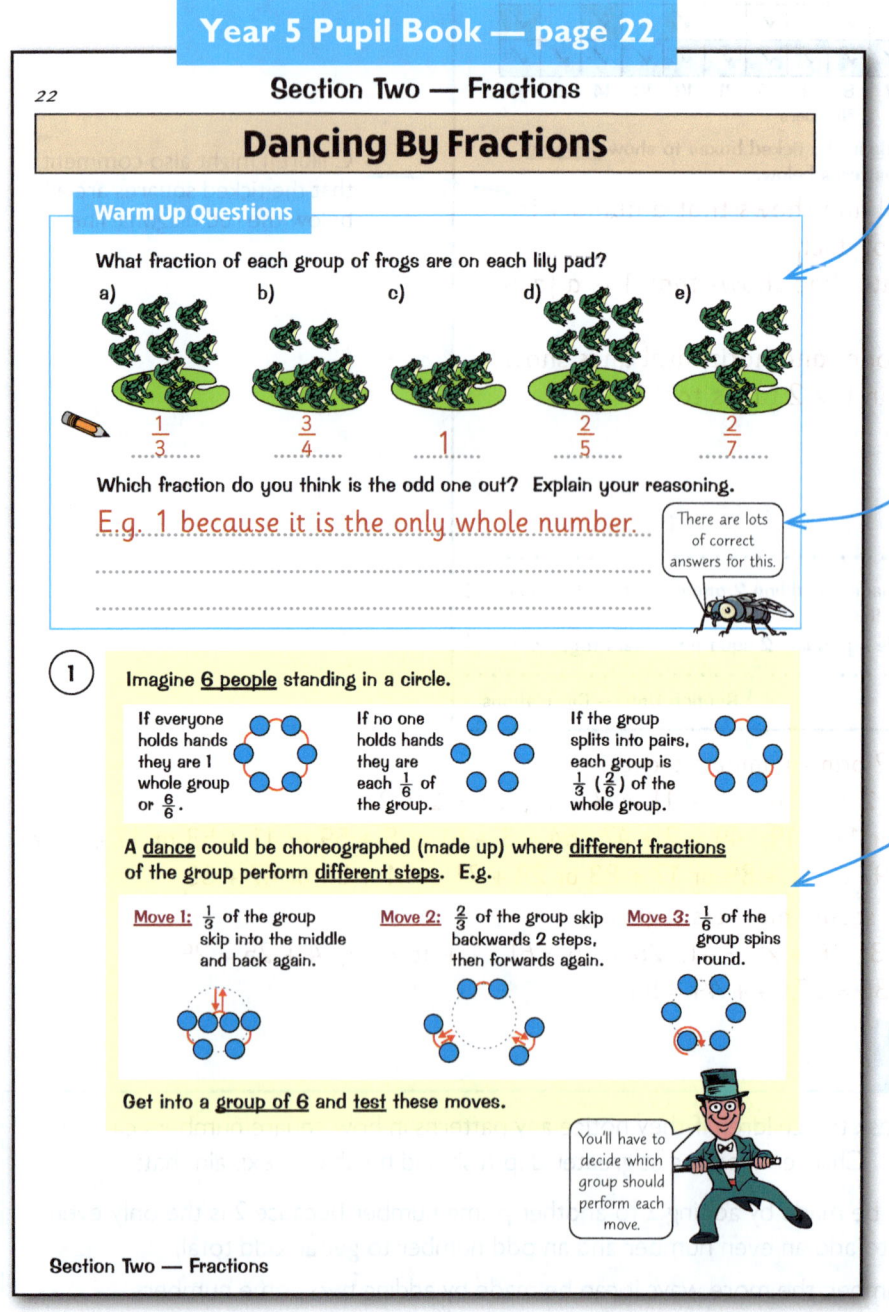

Any equivalent fraction is acceptable. Some children may write $\frac{3}{9}$ for a), $\frac{6}{8}$ for b), $\frac{5}{5}$ for c) and $\frac{4}{10}$ for d). However, if children are able to, they should be encouraged to simplify fractions.

Children are likely to come up with a range of reasoning as to why they think their chosen fraction is the odd one out. E.g. they may choose:

- $\frac{1}{3}$ as it is the only unit fraction.
- $\frac{2}{7}$ because it is the only fraction that cannot be simplified from the numbers shown in the picture.

- This could first be done as a demonstration to the class using 6 of the children with the teacher acting as the choreographer.

- If the class cannot easily be split into groups of 6, this activity could be done one group at a time at the front of the class, with different individuals getting to have a go (and some pupils having to go more than once). Alternatively, pupils could still get into groups of more than 6, and do the dance multiple times so everyone gets to be involved.

- The steps could be repeated so that each child gets to do each step. For example, for Step 1, the first third move to the centre of the circle and return to their places, then the second third do this, then the final third. For step 2, each third will take it in turns to stand still.

Key Stage 2 Maths Investigations — Year 5

Dancing By Fractions

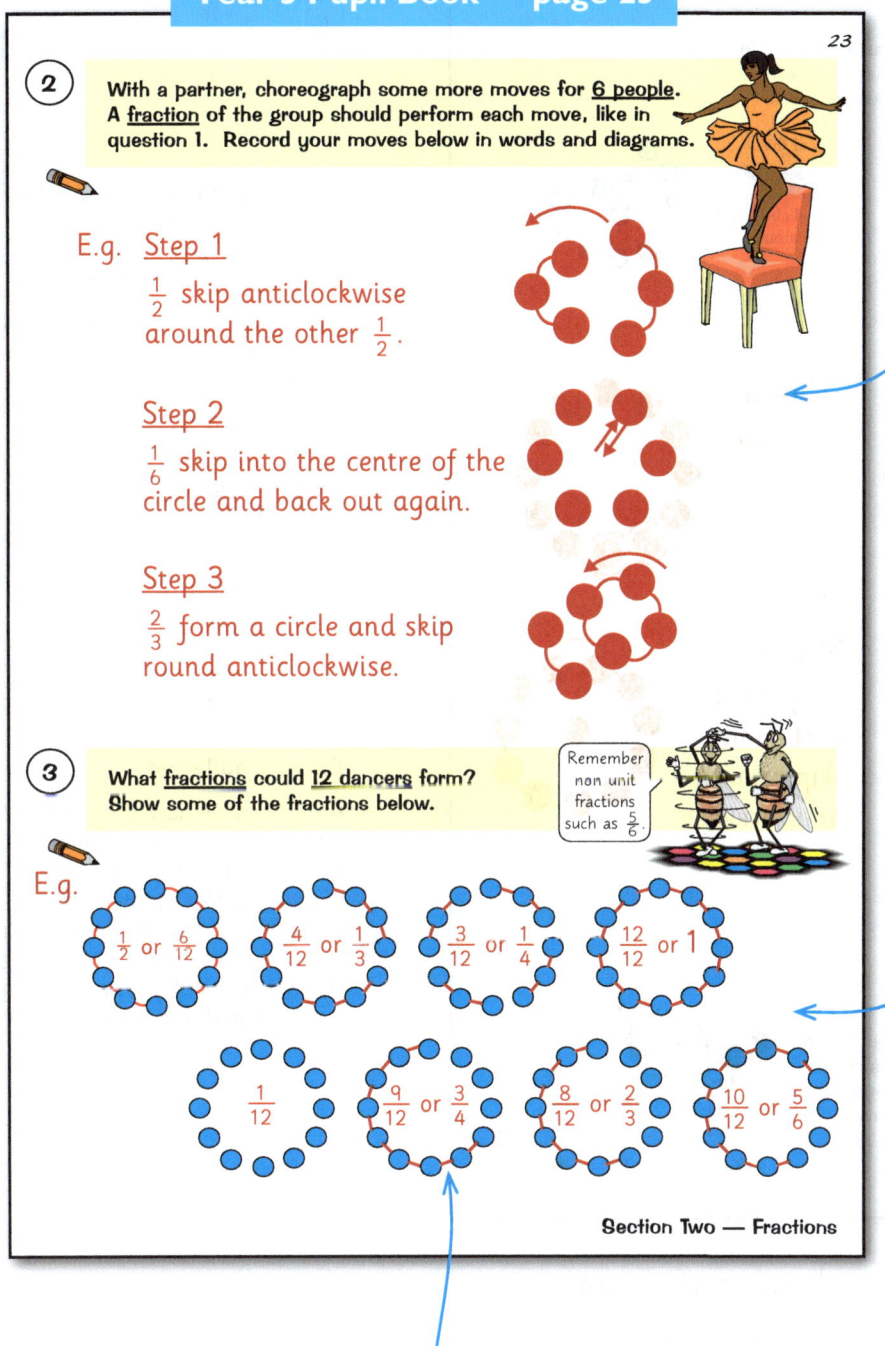

Year 5 Pupil Book — page 23

Extra Support
- Some children may need help with thinking of dance moves (and not necessarily help with the fractions).
- Keep any suggestions simple so the focus remains the number of groups and the number of children in each group.

Children may decide to repeat the moves so that each child/group does each move.

- Encourage children to link groups to factor pairs, e.g. 12 × 1 = 12: 12 groups of 1 or 1 group of 12.
- Other fractions are $\frac{1}{6}$ ($\frac{2}{12}$), $\frac{5}{12}$, $\frac{7}{12}$, $\frac{11}{12}$.
- Children might find it easier to find the unit fractions first, then work systematically to find the non-unit fractions by increasing the numerator.

Some children might find it easier to draw a ring around the correct number of circles to show a fraction, rather than linking the circles with lines.

Key Stage 2 Maths Investigations — Year 5

Dancing By Fractions

Year 5 Pupil Book — page 24

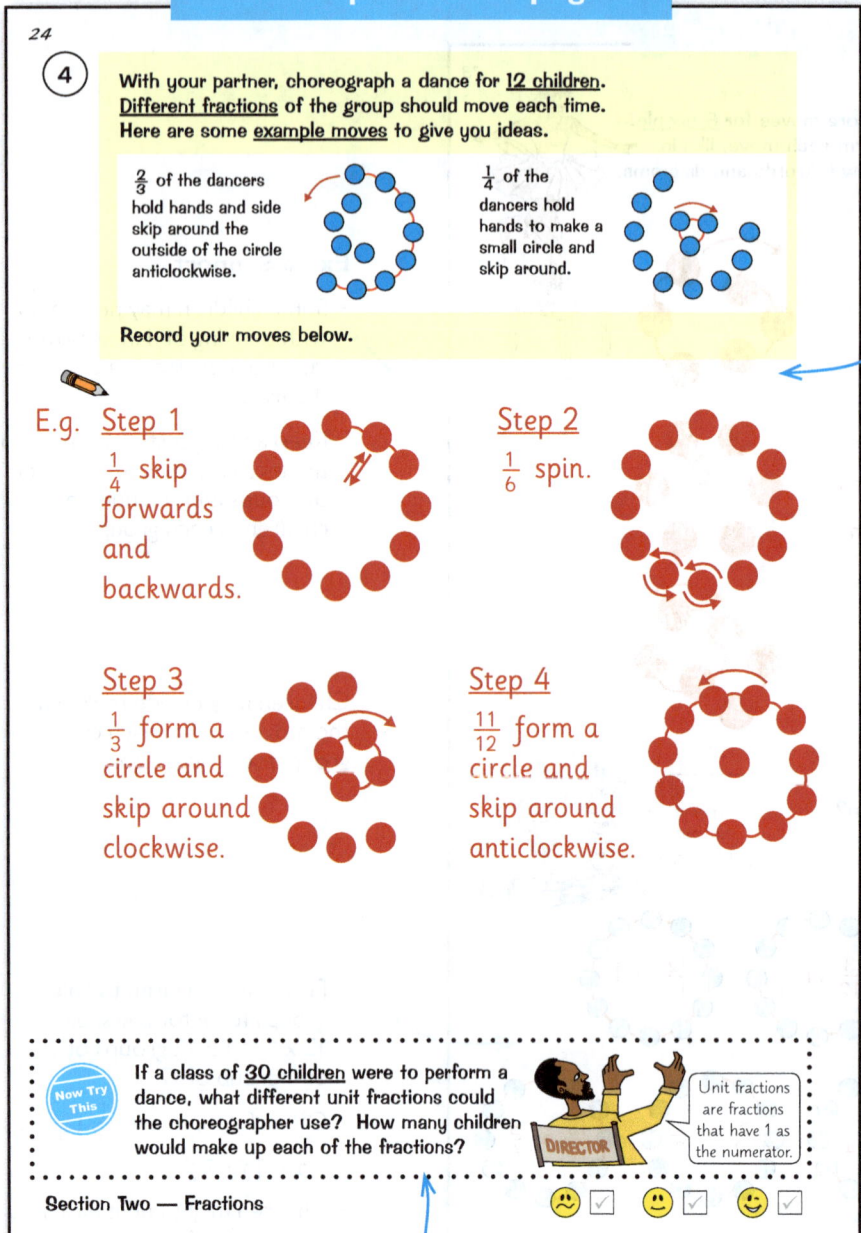

- It will be useful to number the children around the circle, and always start forming groups clockwise from Child 1.
- Groups could perform to each other and children in the audience for each group could try to work out the fractions being used for each step.
- Music could be used to add some fun.

Extra Challenge

After children have devised their moves, some children could try to teach their moves to a group of twelve children. Be sure to remind them to use mathematical language in their instructions, e.g. "One quarter of you need to skip forwards and backwards".

$\frac{1}{30}$ (1 in each group) $\frac{1}{5}$ (6 in each group)

$\frac{1}{15}$ (2 in each group) $\frac{1}{3}$ (10 in each group)

$\frac{1}{10}$ (3 in each group) $\frac{1}{2}$ (15 in each group)

$\frac{1}{6}$ (5 in each group)   1 (30 in the group)

Showing Greater Depth

Children who are working at Greater Depth will be able to:
- (Warm Up part 2) analyse the set of fractions and identify reasons why different fractions may be considered the odd one out. Coming up with a reason for more than one fraction will require them to think about them creatively, in more than one way.

Key Stage 2 Maths Investigations — Year 5

Dominoes and Fractions

Children need to be familiar with unit fractions and non-unit fractions with common denominators. They'll be creating their own fraction wall as a series of number lines showing families of common equivalent fractions. They'll use their fraction wall to generate comparisons between different fractions. Then, they will explore the decimals of the fractions, and come up with rules about recurring decimals.

Aims:

- Measure accurately using centimetres and millimetres.
- Recognise and show, using visual diagrams, families of common equivalent fractions.
- Compare fractions using families of common equivalent fractions using =, < and >.
- Explore which fractions give recurring decimals.

Key Vocabulary:

'numerator', 'denominator', 'equivalent fractions', 'recurring decimal'

Resources Needed:

A set of dominoes per pair, calculator
Printable dominoes are available at:
cgpbooks.co.uk/KS2-Maths-Investigations

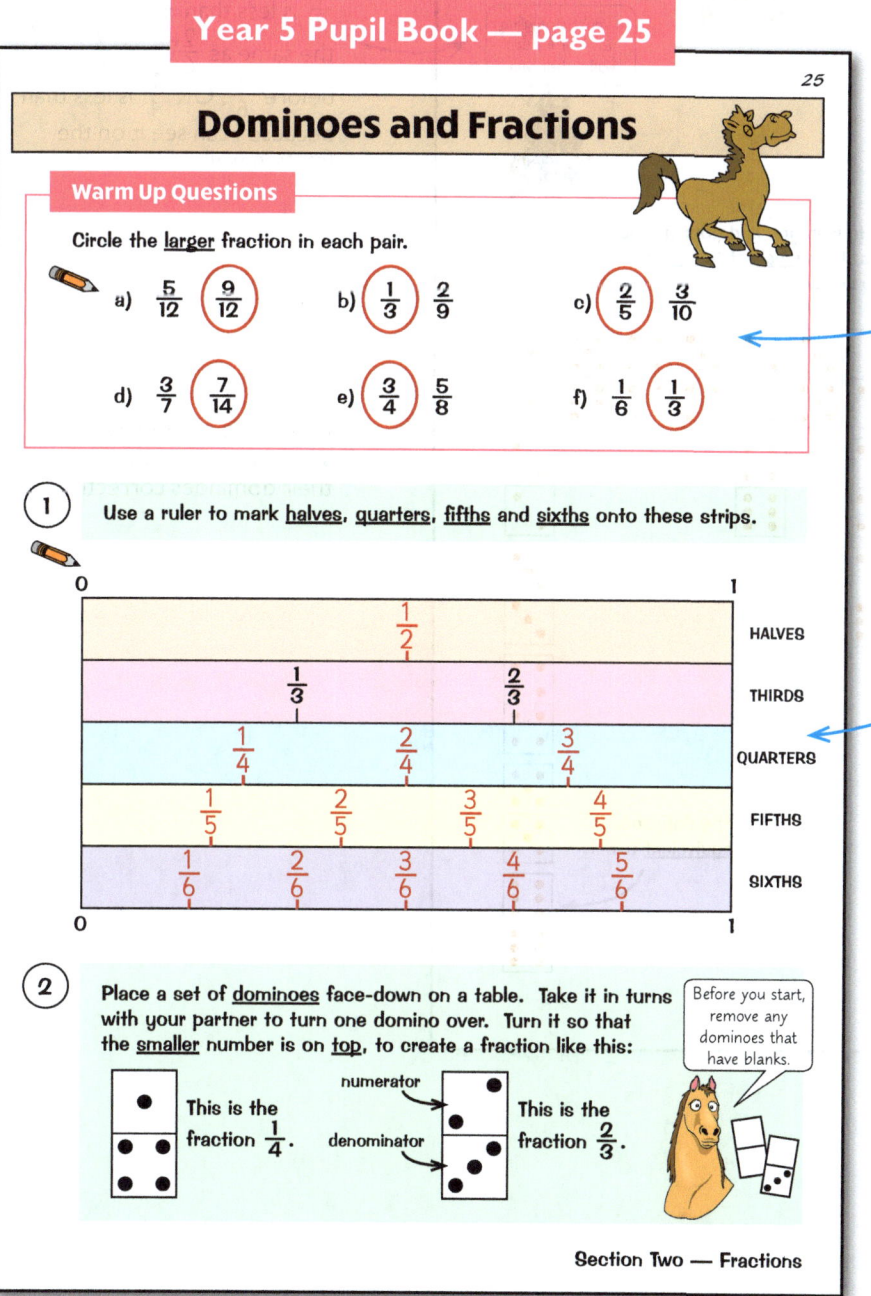

Remind children to look at the relationship between the denominators to compare each pair of fractions.

- Make sure the unit fractions create a diagonal line showing clearly that $\frac{1}{2} > \frac{1}{3} > \frac{1}{4}$ etc., the intervals are evenly spaced and equivalent fractions are lined up.

- Encourage children to use a ruler to measure the strips and then divide this length by 2, 4, 5 or 6.

Dominoes and Fractions

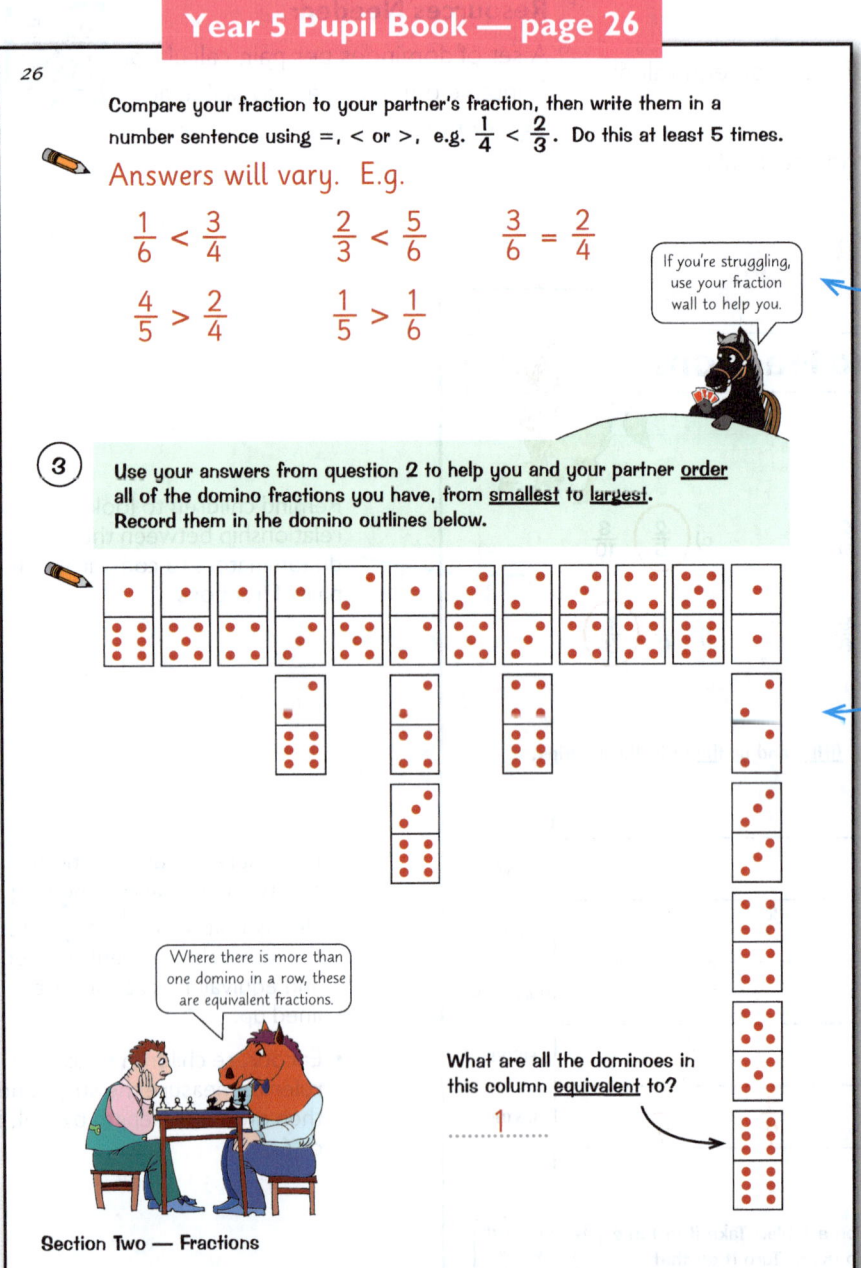

Year 5 Pupil Book — page 26

Partner work will encourage the children to discuss how they are comparing their fractions, e.g. $\frac{1}{3}$ is less than $\frac{3}{6}$ because $\frac{1}{3}$ is the same as $\frac{2}{6}$, and $\frac{2}{6}$ comes before $\frac{3}{6}$, OR $\frac{1}{4}$ is less than $\frac{2}{6}$ because I can see it on the fraction wall.

Encourage children to work systematically so that they order their dominoes correctly

Dominoes and Fractions

Year 5 Pupil Book — page 27

④ Some fractions give recurring decimals. This means they go on forever with repeated digits, like this: $\frac{1}{3}$ = 0.33333333333333333333... Investigate which dominoes give recurring decimals. Try to come up with a rule, and then test it.

If you can't work out the decimal, use a calculator.

Recurring	Not recurring
$\frac{1}{3}$ $\frac{2}{3}$	$\frac{1}{1}$ $\frac{1}{2}$ $\frac{2}{2}$ $\frac{3}{3}$ $\frac{1}{4}$ $\frac{2}{4}$ $\frac{3}{4}$ $\frac{4}{4}$
$\frac{1}{6}$ $\frac{2}{6}$ $\frac{4}{6}$ $\frac{5}{6}$	$\frac{1}{5}$ $\frac{2}{5}$ $\frac{3}{5}$ $\frac{4}{5}$ $\frac{5}{5}$ $\frac{3}{6}$ $\frac{6}{6}$

Rule: E.g. Fractions that give recurring decimals will have a 3 or a 6 as a denominator. They will also have a numerator which is not a 3 or a 6.

Show your thinking

Explain your rule, how you tested it and what you've discovered.

E.g. the only domino fractions that give recurring decimals had either 3 or 6 as a denominator, so at first I thought that was the rule. But then I tested it with $\frac{3}{6}$ and found that it makes 0.5. Also, $\frac{3}{3}$ and $\frac{6}{6}$ make 1. So I changed my rule to make sure those were not included.

Now Try This: Sort your dominoes into families of denominators, e.g. quarters, sixths etc. Select two dominoes from each family and add them. If they make an improper fraction, convert it into a mixed number. Repeat with two new dominoes. What's the largest mixed number you can create?

Section Two — Fractions

Answers will vary, e.g.
$\frac{3}{5} + \frac{4}{5} = \frac{7}{5} = \frac{5}{5} + \frac{2}{5} = 1\frac{2}{5}$

The largest mixed number you can create will be:
$\frac{5}{6} + \frac{6}{6} = \frac{11}{6} = 1\frac{5}{6}$

- Be prepared to give children a couple more examples of recurring decimals as this is a new concept for them.
- Children could divide their page into two columns — fractions which give recurring decimals, and fractions which give non-recurring (terminating) decimals.
- Some children should be able to find recurring decimals by the short division method, e.g. for $\frac{1}{6}$:
$$6\overline{)1.0^{1}0^{4}0^{4}0^{4}0} = 0.1666...$$

Extra Challenge
- Ask pupils to explore other numbers — not just using the dominoes. Does their rule still hold?
- In fact, the full rule is this: For a fraction not to be recurring (i.e. terminating), the fraction in its simplest form must have a denominator with prime factors of 2s and 5s only. All other fractions will give recurring decimals.

  E.g. Not recurring (terminating):
  $\frac{2}{5}, \frac{1}{2}, \frac{3}{4}$ (4 = 2 × 2 (or 2^2)),
  $\frac{7}{10}$ (10 = 5 × 2),
  $\frac{6}{15}$ (can be simplified to $\frac{2}{5}$)
  Recurring: $\frac{2}{3}, \frac{4}{7}, \frac{6}{11}, \frac{1}{90}$
  (90 = 3^2 × 5 × 2, so prime factors are not 2s and 5s only)

- It's highly unlikely pupils will come up with this full rule, but encourage them to write down the factors of the denominators and see what they notice.

Showing Greater Depth

Children working at Greater Depth will be able to:

- (Q4) ensure their rule takes account of dominoes such as $\frac{3}{3}$ and $\frac{3}{6}$, which can be simplified to give terminating fractions or whole numbers. They will demonstrate they have tested their rule, then refined it and re-tested it.

A Thousand Paces

In this investigation, children will begin by estimating how many steps there are from their home to their school. They will then be given more information on how many steps they might take in a given distance, and measure how long their steps are, in order to come up with a more accurate estimate.

Aims:

- Round numbers to given powers of 10 and 1 decimal place.
- Solve practical but relatable problems.
- Convert between metric units.
- Consider the relationship between metric and other units (imperial and non-standard).

Key Vocabulary:
'mile', 'kilometre', 'metre', 'centimetre', 'estimate'

Resources Needed:
Access to the internet, metre ruler/tape measure, calculator

Year 5 Pupil Book — page 28

Section Three — Measurement and Geometry

A Thousand Paces

Warm Up Questions

1) Match the numbers in the circle to the nearest 10. The first one has been done for you.

   Numbers in circle: 60, 10, 62, 12.6, 45, 30, 104.7, 40, 110, 91.99, 38.4, 105.1, 34.87, 100, 50, 90

2) Match the numbers in the circle to the nearest hundred. The first one has been done for you.

   Numbers in circle: 1200, 300, 900, 345.5, 979, 405, 229.9, 800, 1100, 1058, 848.7, 1184, 200, 909.9, 400, 1000

(1) Estimate how many steps you think you would take to walk from your home to school.

What have you based your estimate on? Discuss it with a partner.

I estimate I take **Answers will vary** steps from my home to school.

Section Three — Measurement and Geometry

The important thing here is to encourage children to use some form of reasoning, or 'sense checking'. E.g. children may say: "It takes me about 20 minutes to walk to school, and I probably do about X steps per minute. Therefore..." Encourage children to follow their logic through as far as they can.

A Thousand Paces

29

Year 5 Pupil Book — page 29

 ② Use the internet to find out how far in <u>miles</u> it is from your <u>home</u> to your <u>school</u>.

Although we usually use the metric system to measure things (m, cm, kg, ml etc.), we still often use miles for large distances.

E.g.
I live <u>1.8</u> miles from school.

 ③ The word 'mile' comes from the Latin phrase 'mille passus', which means 'a thousand paces'. It was a measure of distance for the marching Roman army. 'Left and right' counted as one 'passus' though, so really it was <u>2000 steps</u>.

Use this information to make a new estimate for the number of steps from your home to school.

E.g. 1.8 miles × 2000 steps per mile = 3600 steps

 My new estimate for the number of steps from home to school is <u>3600</u>.

Show your thinking

 Do you think this estimate is accurate? Or might it be an <u>over</u>estimate, or an <u>under</u>estimate? Explain your thinking below.

E.g. The average Roman soldier would have been taller than me and so was likely to have taken longer steps. This would mean I would need to take more steps, so my estimate in Q3 is probably an <u>under</u>estimate.

Section Three — Measurement and Geometry

- If access to the internet for the whole class is not possible, this could be pre-prepared for the children or set as research homework prior to the investigation.

- Children may need to round their answer. 1 decimal place is sensible. (They will need to do further calculations with this number, and more decimal places make those calculations unnecessarily complicated!)

Children may also comment that the way in which the distance is measured by the internet tool might not accurately reflect the number of steps needed. E.g.

- Children may not always be able to walk in a straight line (the most direct route).

- They may take a short cut that the internet calculation doesn't take into account.

- They may have to make more short steps at some points of the journey, e.g. to go through a gate or down an uneven path.

These are valid observations, but the remainder of the investigation deals with their personal step size, so try to elicit the idea of the importance of step size from all children before they move on.

Key Stage 2 Maths Investigations — Year 5

A Thousand Paces

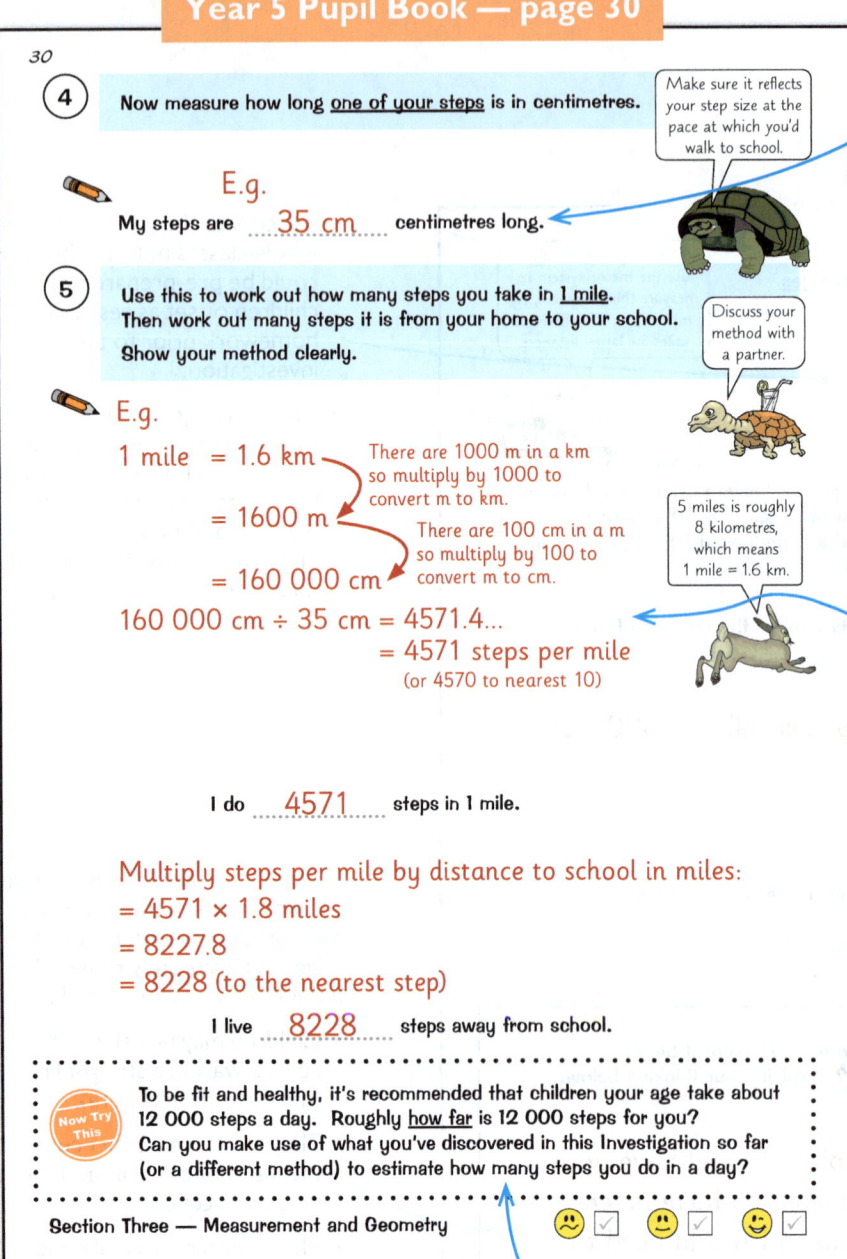

Year 5 Pupil Book — page 30

Encourage children to give their answer to the nearest centimetre here, otherwise the calculations will get too complicated.

Extra Challenge

Instead of just taking a randomly-sized step and measuring it, children may devise a better method to measure their average step length when walking at a normal pace. E.g. mark out a stretch of classroom which is 5 m long. Children walk this 5 m stretch at the pace they would walk to school and count the steps. Then they divide 500 cm by the number of steps to give a fairly accurate average step length.

Suggest to students that they should use a calculator from this point.

Discuss rounding in this question.
- Any numbers after the decimal point represent less than 1 step, so they should be rounded up or down.
- Rounding to 2 significant figures is a fairly standard degree of accuracy, so you may ask students to round their answer to the nearest 100 steps.

Students can compare their final answer with what they estimated at the start of the investigation. Whose original estimation was the closest to their final answer?

- To find how far 12 000 steps is for them in cm, children can multiply the length of their step by 12 000. They should then convert the length to metres and kilometres.
- Children who walk to and from school could double their answer to Q5, then consider how many other steps they do in a day, e.g. at playtime.
- Children may decide that it's not appropriate to work out their daily number of steps by distance walked because of all the short steps they do — they may decide to use different reasoning, e.g. 'I'm on my feet for about 2 hours a day, and I probably do x steps per minute...'
- Whatever train of logic they use, encourage them to take it as far as they can.

E.g. 35 cm × 12 000 = 420 000 cm = 4200 m = 4.2 km
On days when I walk to and from school, I walk 16 456 steps just during those journeys, and then I think I do about 4000 more steps in the rest of the day (20 456 in total). When I get a lift to school and from school, I will walk less, although I then have more time after school to play football, which involves a lot of steps. On those days, I think I do about 9000 steps.

Showing Greater Depth

Children working at Greater Depth will be able to:
- (Q3 Show Your Thinking) realise and account for the fact that not all steps that they take will be an equal length — e.g. shorter steps going uphill and downhill, longer steps when running, etc.

Key Stage 2 Maths Investigations — Year 5

Quadrilateral Areas

In this investigation, children will create different quadrilaterals on 9-pin pegboards, then work out their areas. They'll then investigate how area is affected by increasing the size of the quadrilaterals by a particular scale factor. Children should know the names of different quadrilaterals, and how to find an area by counting squares.

Aims:

- Calculate areas of irregular shapes.
- Identify all the possible different quadrilaterals.
- Enlarge a shape by a given scale factor.

Key Vocabulary:

'quadrilateral', 'parallelogram', 'square', 'trapezium', 'rectangle', 'kite', 'inverted kite', 'area', 'scale factor'

Resources Needed:

Rulers, pegboards and elastic bands (or printed versions of pegboards). Printable pegboards are available at cgpbooks.co.uk/KS2-Maths-Investigations

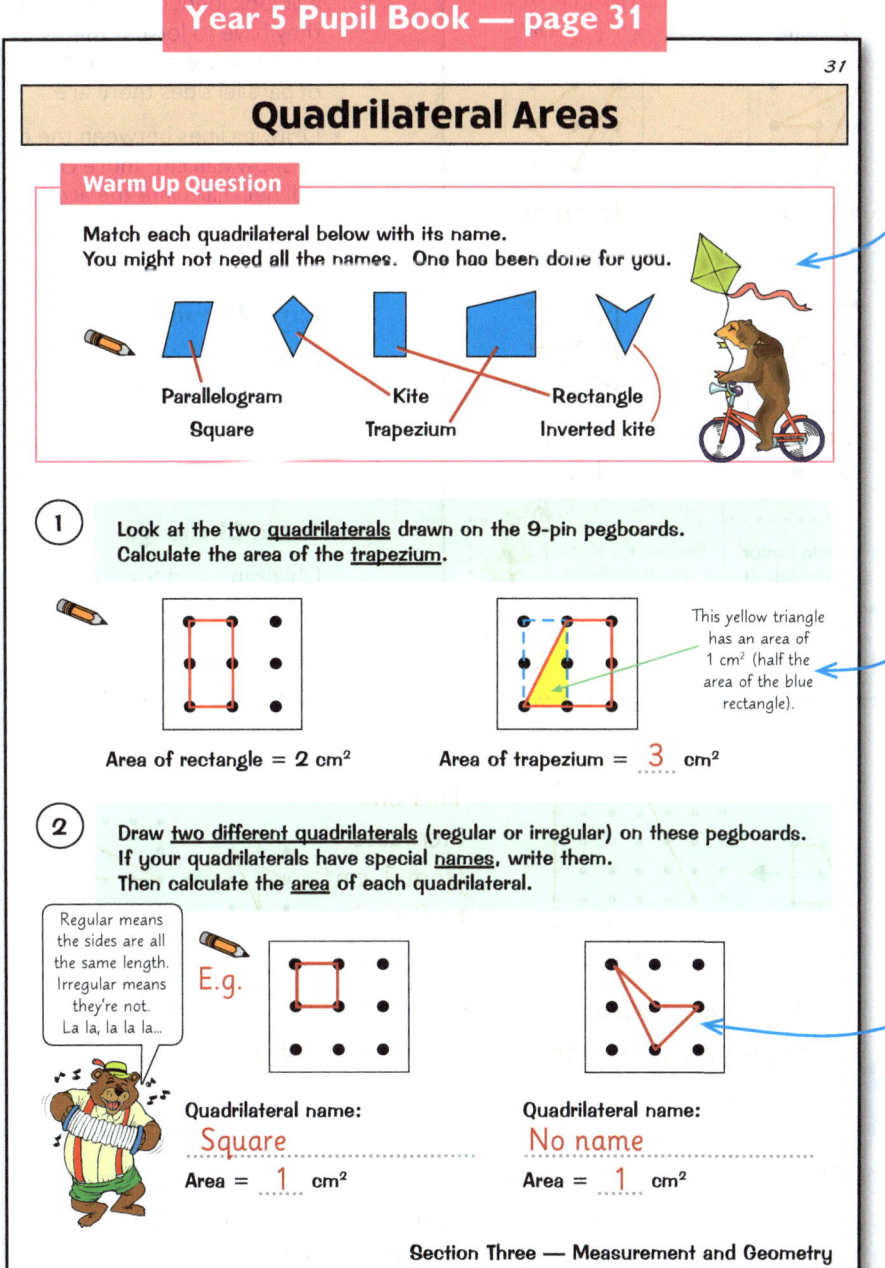

- Encourage children to name the shapes they definitely know first (process of elimination) and then look for clues to help identify the remaining shapes.
- Although children are more likely to use the obvious labels, be aware that, technically, a rectangle is a special type of parallelogram.

Extra Support

If children struggle to see that the triangle part of the trapezium is equivalent to 1 cm², let them draw it on a separate piece of paper with exact measurements. If they cut out the blue rectangle (as shown in the question) and then cut the diagonal they will see that the 2 triangles they have made are identical and therefore each have an area of 1 cm².

For smaller shapes, like this one, it can be easier to work out the area not in the shape. E.g.

- The whole pegboard has an area of 4 cm².
- The area not within the quadrilateral is 1 + 0.5 + 0.5 + 1 (half of 2) = 3 cm².
- Therefore the area within the quadrilateral is 4 − 3 = 1 cm².

Key Stage 2 Maths Investigations — Year 5

Quadrilateral Areas

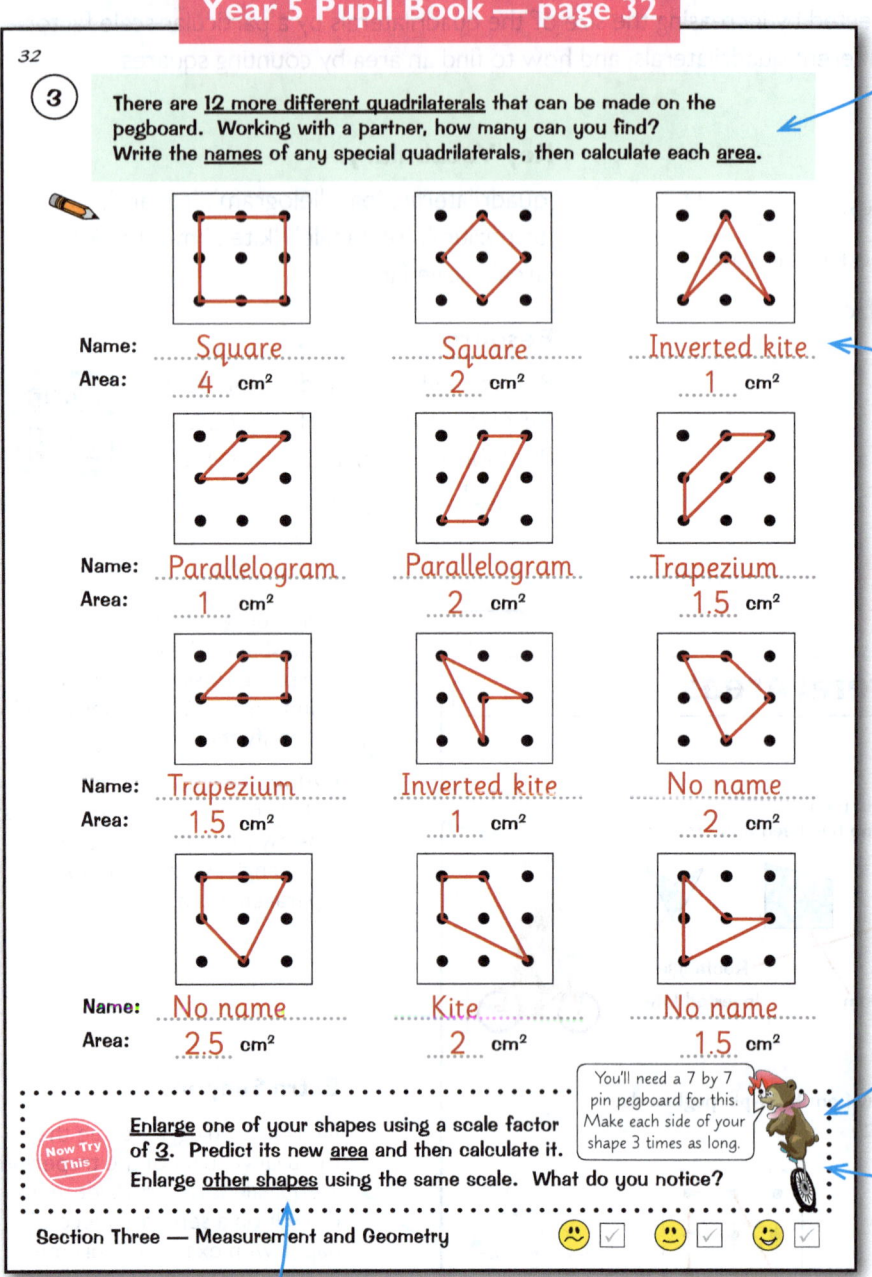

- Using an actual 9-pin pegboard and an elastic band to create each shape (instead of just a diagram) will allow children to experiment with shapes more easily and therefore instigate greater discussion.

- Some children might include reflections as a different shape. This isn't necessarily wrong, and is an interesting topic for discussion.

- Remind children to refer back to the Warm Up Questions to see the names of quadrilaterals.

- However, children need to be aware that not every trapezium, inverted kite, etc., will look identical. Therefore, they have to look at the properties, e.g. how many pairs of parallel sides there are.

- Drawing lines between the pins to show half cm² more clearly will help calculate the area.

Extra Support
Encourage children to choose easy shapes (e.g. squares or rectangles) so it's easier to find the area once enlarged.

Extra Challenge
Children could try using different scale factors. A scale factor of 2 will make the area 4 times bigger (2 × 2), and a scale factor of 4 will make the area 16 times bigger (4 × 4).

E.g.
I think the area of the shape on the right will be 3 × 3 = 9 cm² when enlarged.

It's actually 27 cm²

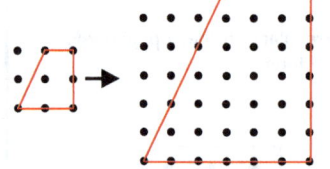

This one increases from 1 cm² to 9 cm²

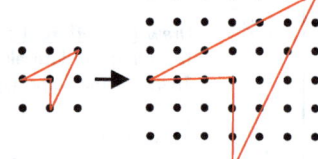

The area of each shape became 9 times bigger when enlarged by a scale factor of 3.

Showing Greater Depth

Children working at Greater Depth will be able to:
- (Q3) explain to a partner why a shape is the same as one already recorded, i.e. whether it has been shifted on the grid (translated), turned around (rotated) or flipped over (reflected).

Key Stage 2 Maths Investigations — Year 5

Tessellations

Children will identify shapes that do and don't tessellate and explain why. They'll use regular 2D shapes to investigate which ones tessellate. They'll then investigate what combinations of shapes can semi-tessellate. By looking at angles around a point, they'll identify shapes that can and can't tessellate around a point.

Aims:

- Draw tessellating shapes accurately.
- Distinguish between regular and irregular polygons.
- Recognise the relationship between angles and a whole turn; use this knowledge in further reasoning.

Key Vocabulary:

'tessellation', 'regular', 'semi-tessellation', 'interior angles'

Resources Needed:

Spare paper, 2D shapes — if needed, there are a set of 2D shapes that could be printed on card and handed out for children to use and draw around at cgpbooks.co.uk/KS2-Maths-Investigations

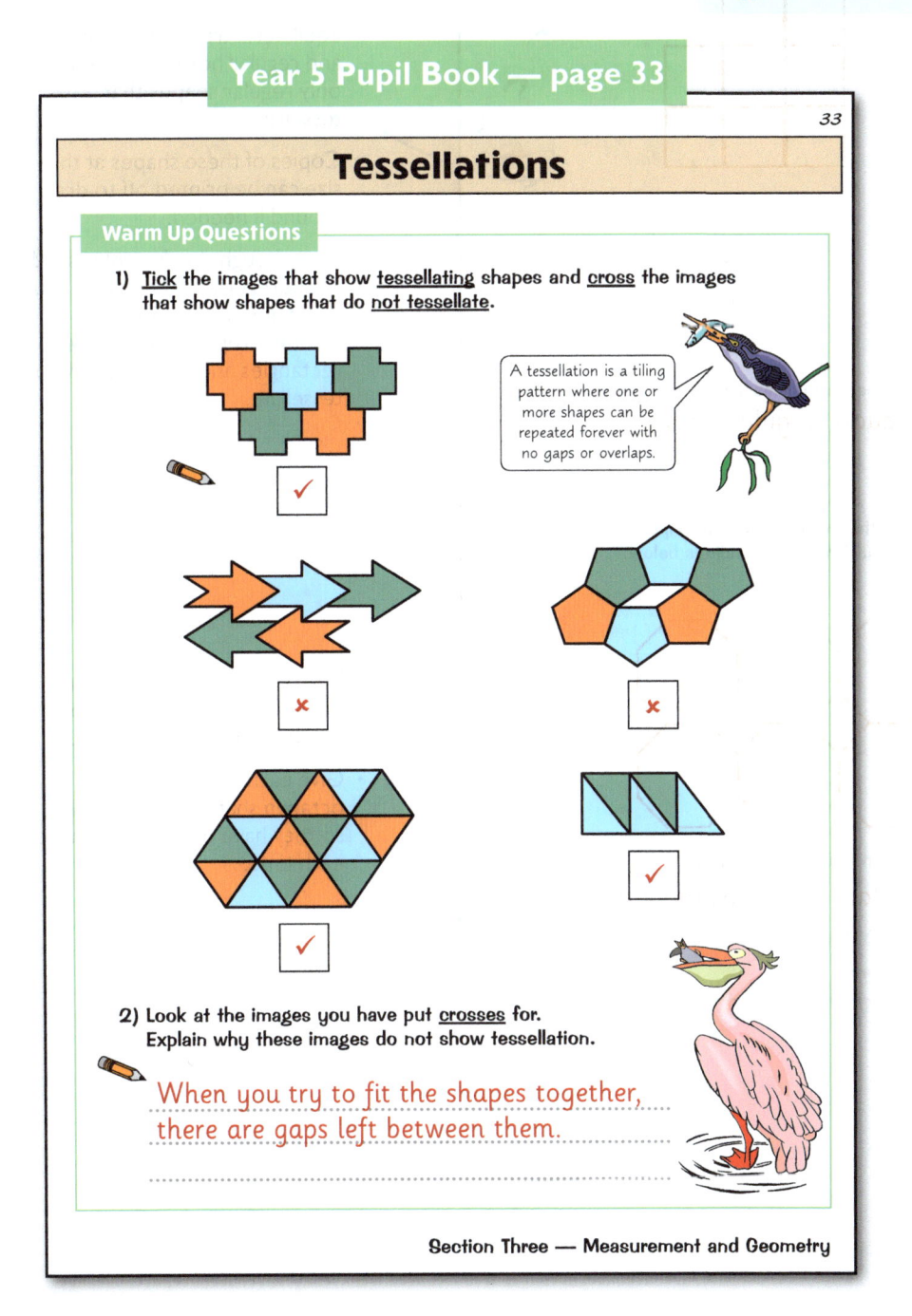

Year 5 Pupil Book — page 33

Tessellations

Warm Up Questions

1) Tick the images that show tessellating shapes and cross the images that show shapes that do not tessellate.

A tessellation is a tiling pattern where one or more shapes can be repeated forever with no gaps or overlaps.

2) Look at the images you have put crosses for. Explain why these images do not show tessellation.

When you try to fit the shapes together, there are gaps left between them.

Section Three — Measurement and Geometry

Key Stage 2 Maths Investigations — Year 5

Tessellations

Year 5 Pupil Book — page 34

① Using regular 2D shapes only, investigate which ones tessellate. For the shapes below that tessellate, draw more copies of each shape to show evidence of your findings.

In regular shapes, the sides are all the same length and the angles are all equal.

E.g.

Write the names of the regular shapes that tessellate.
equilateral triangle, square, regular hexagon

② Work with a partner. Work together to find out what happens when you try to tessellate regular octagons. Draw your findings below.

Describe what has happened when you tried to tessellate regular octagons.
When you try to tessellate octagons, there are square-shaped gaps left in between them.

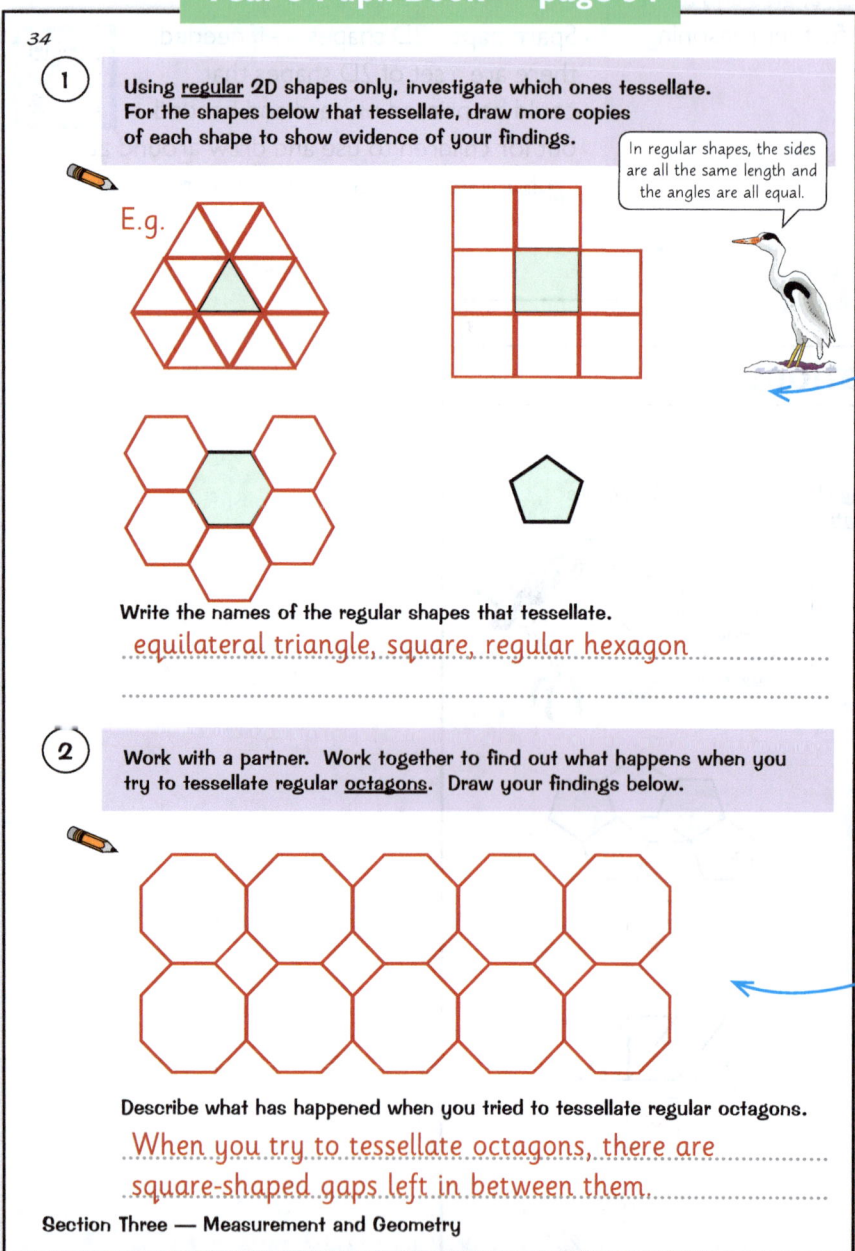

Section Three — Measurement and Geometry

- Equilateral triangles, squares and regular hexagons are the only regular shapes that tessellate.
- Copies of these shapes at this size can be printed off to draw around if needed.
- Even though they're only asked about regular shapes here, you could also ask children to identify irregular shapes like rectangles and diamonds that tessellate.

- The online resource contains octagons small enough to be drawn around in this space.
- Give each child just one octagon shape to work with, so they have to draw around it each time.

Tessellations

Year 5 Pupil Book — page 35

③ You should have seen in question 2 that a second shape was needed for the octagons to tessellate. When 2 or more different shapes tessellate, it is called a semi-tessellation. Investigate which combinations of 2D shapes work to create semi-tessellations. Record your findings below.

Answers will vary. E.g.

You could start by trying to tessellate one shape and seeing what shapes are left in the gaps.

④ The 3 shapes below tessellate. Look at their interior angles around a point.

Interior angle = 90°   Interior angle = 60°   Interior angle = 120°

Why do you think these shapes tessellate around a point?
They tessellate around a point because the interior angle of each shape is a factor of 360°, i.e. 90° × 4 = 360°, 60° × 6 = 360° and 120° × 3 = 360°.

Section Three — Measurement and Geometry

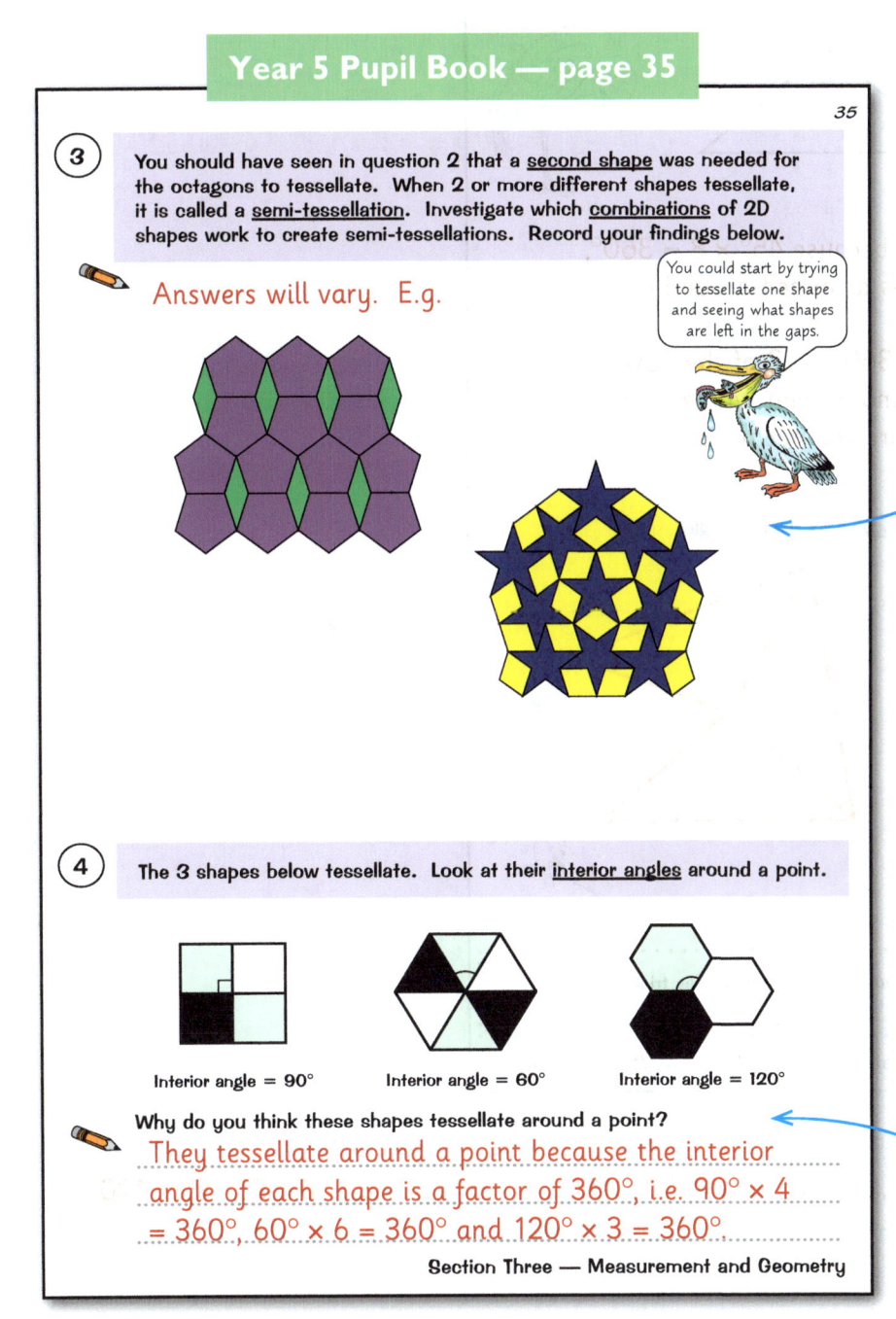

- For this activity, it is a good idea for children to use 2D shapes to tessellate so they can easily manipulate the overall pattern they are making. These could be plastic shapes if available in the classroom, or card shapes printed off and cut out from the online resource, or even shapes that children have made themselves.

- When they are satisfied they have created a semi-tessellation, they can record it by drawing around the outside of each shape (this is likely to need a spare piece of paper for space).

- Possible pairs of shapes include: pentagons with rhombuses, five-pointed stars with rhombuses, and (as shown in the previous answer) octagons with squares.

- The side lengths of all shapes need to be the same.

Extra Support

You might need to remind children that the angles around a point add up to 360° in total.

This question will encourage children to look carefully and see the connection between each of the tessellations: that their repeated interior angles add up to 360°.

Key Stage 2 Maths Investigations — Year 5

Tessellations

Year 5 Pupil Book — page 36

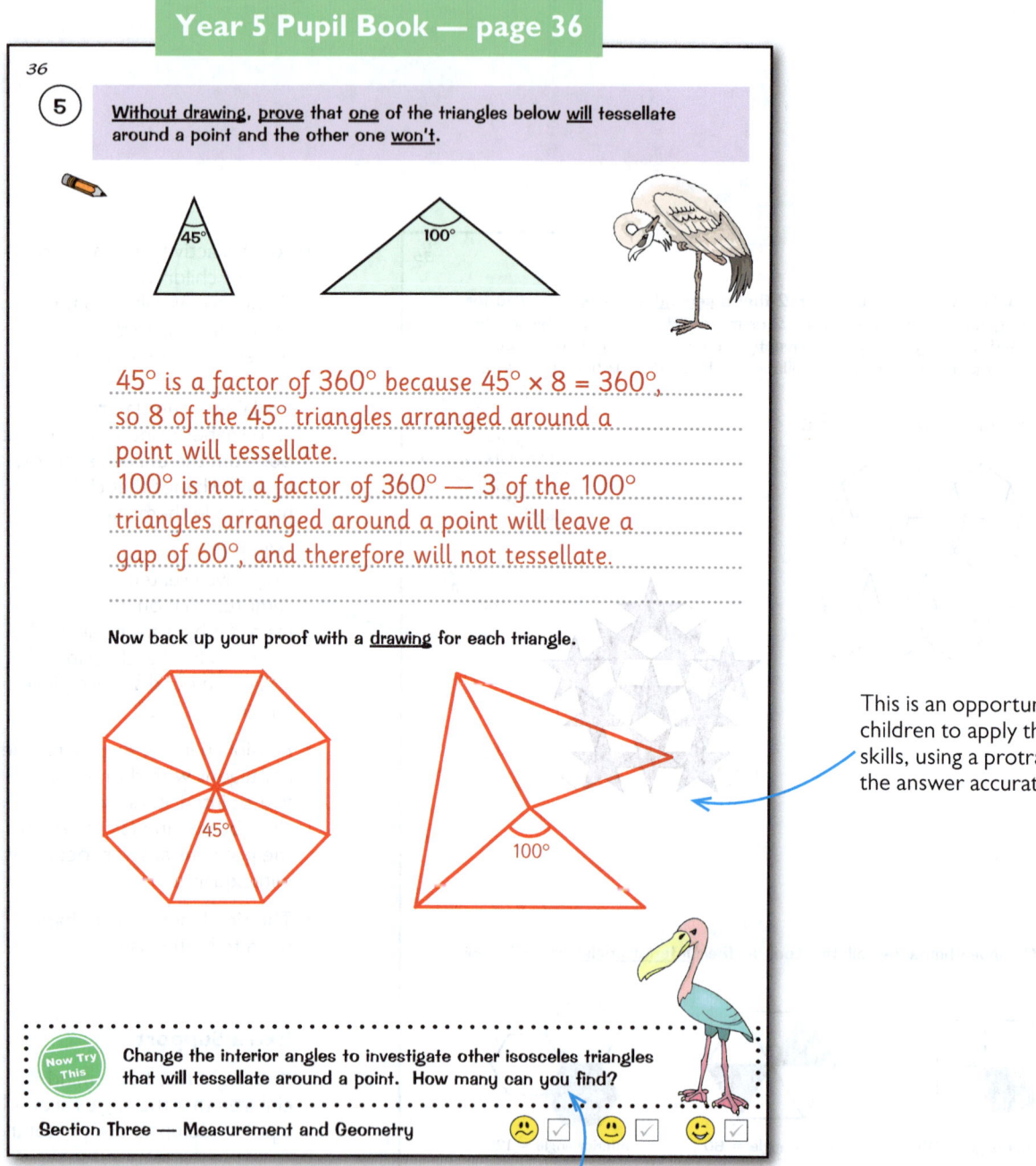

5 Without drawing, prove that one of the triangles below will tessellate around a point and the other one won't.

45° is a factor of 360° because 45° × 8 = 360°, so 8 of the 45° triangles arranged around a point will tessellate.
100° is not a factor of 360° — 3 of the 100° triangles arranged around a point will leave a gap of 60°, and therefore will not tessellate.

Now back up your proof with a drawing for each triangle.

> This is an opportunity for children to apply their drawing skills, using a protractor to show the answer accurately.

Now Try This: Change the interior angles to investigate other isosceles triangles that will tessellate around a point. How many can you find?

Section Three — Measurement and Geometry

Answers will vary but the non-repeated interior angle of the isosceles triangle will need to be one of the following:
1°, 2°, 3°, 4°, 5°, 6°, 8°, 9°, 10°, 12°, 15°, 18°, 20°, 24°, 30°, 36°, 40°, 45°, 60°, 72°, 90°, 120°
Children can use knowledge of times tables, factors and trial and improvement to find out some of these answers.

Showing Greater Depth

Children working at Greater Depth will be able to:
- (Q5) apply what they noticed about the tessellating shapes in question 4 (i.e. that the interior angles are factors of 360°) to work out what will happen to the isosceles triangles, without having to model or draw them first.

Triangle Transformations

Children need to recognise triangles and be able to name them. They'll be performing different transformations: translations, rotations about different vertex points, and reflections through various lines of symmetry. They'll be comparing transformations and looking for patterns in the results.

Aims:

- Classify triangles based on their properties.
- Identify and represent the position of a shape following a translation, rotation or reflection.
- Compare transformations and notice patterns.

Key Vocabulary:

'translation', 'rotation', 'reflection', 'vertex', 'equilateral', 'isosceles', 'scalene'

Resources Needed:

Ruler, colouring pencils, protractor, tracing paper, mirror.

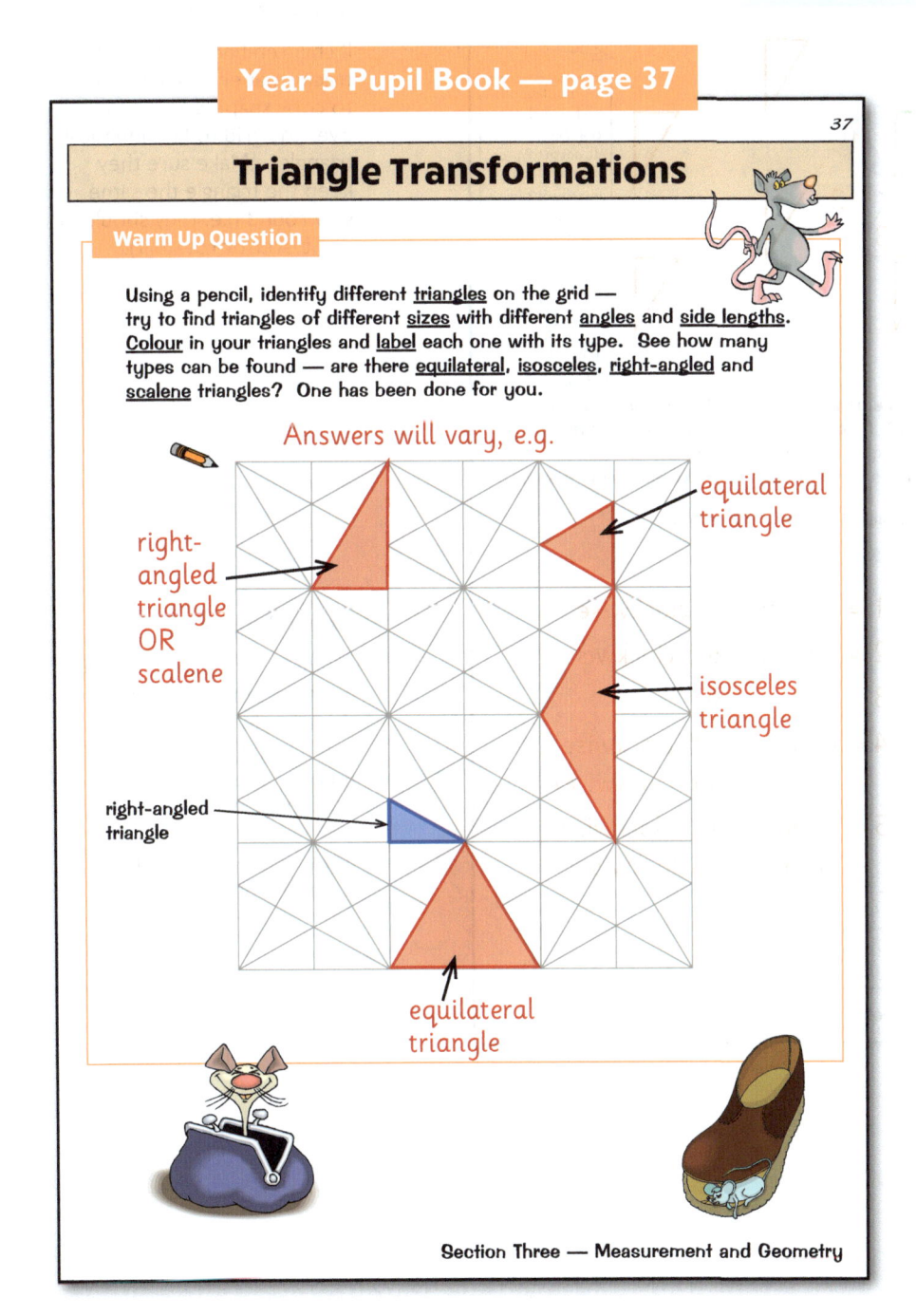

Year 5 Pupil Book — page 37

Triangle Transformations

Warm Up Question

Using a pencil, identify different triangles on the grid — try to find triangles of different sizes with different angles and side lengths. Colour in your triangles and label each one with its type. See how many types can be found — are there equilateral, isosceles, right-angled and scalene triangles? One has been done for you.

Answers will vary, e.g.

- right-angled triangle OR scalene
- equilateral triangle
- isosceles triangle
- right-angled triangle
- equilateral triangle

Children might also correctly label right-angled triangles as scalene triangles (scalene triangles can be right-angled and vice versa).

Section Three — Measurement and Geometry

Key Stage 2 Maths Investigations — Year 5

Triangle Transformations

Year 5 Pupil Book — page 38

38

① Look at the shape (S) on the grid below. How many <u>translations</u> can you find on the same grid? <u>Shade</u> all of the translations the same colour.

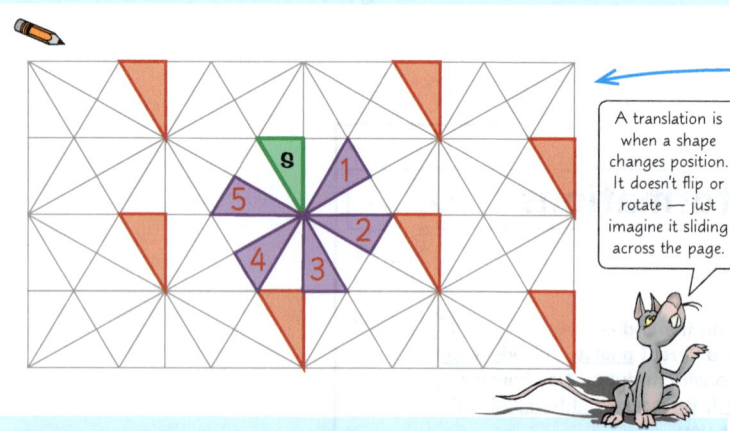

A translation is when a shape changes position. It doesn't flip or rotate — just imagine it sliding across the page.

Extra Support

If children find this difficult, tracing paper could be used to copy shape S and move over the grid to find identical triangles. Make sure they keep the triangle the same way round (i.e. they shouldn't flip it over or rotate it).

② Rotating around the red spot (the centre of rotation), how many different ways can you rotate triangle S? Colour in the rotations using a different colour to your translations from question 1 and number them.
Describe the transformation S has gone through to make each new triangle like this:

Triangle S ⟶ Triangle 1 = rotated 90° clockwise

Triangle S ⟶ Triangle 1 = rotated 60° clockwise

Triangle S ⟶ Triangle 2 = rotated 120° clockwise

Triangle S ⟶ Triangle 3 = rotated 180°

Triangle S ⟶ Triangle 4 = rotated 240° clockwise
(or 120° anti-clockwise)

Triangle S ⟶ Triangle 5 = rotated 300° clockwise
(or 60° anti-clockwise)

Extra Support

Children struggling to work out the number of degrees the triangle has been rotated could begin by counting the number of triangles inside the hexagonal shape (12) — relate this to the clock. If the whole circle is 360°, each section is 30°.

You might want to use tracing paper here — trace the shape, then put your pencil on the red spot and turn the tracing paper around until your triangle lines up with the grid.

Section Three — Measurement and Geometry

Triangle Transformations

Year 5 Pupil Book — page 39

③ What happens if you change the centre of rotation to a different vertex on triangle S and rotate it in different ways? Investigate below.

There are two possible centres of rotation:

Remember to show the centre of rotation with a red spot.

The triangle could be rotated around the top left vertex, shown in blue, or the top right vertex, shown in pink.

Extra Challenge

Ask children how many degrees triangle S has been rotated to make the new shapes. Answers:

- Top right vertex: rotation 180°
- Top left vertex: rotation 120° and 240° clockwise

Show your thinking

Think about what was <u>different</u> and what was the <u>same</u> when you changed the centre of rotation. Write your findings below.

E.g. Different centres of rotation produced different numbers of possible triangles on the grid. There were 5 other triangles when using the bottom vertex, but only 2 others for the top left vertex, and 1 for the top right vertex.

Each group of rotated triangles creates a pattern — the alternating triangles within a certain shape are coloured in. For the bottom vertex, it is a hexagon, for the top left it is an equilateral triangle, and for the top right it is a rhombus.

Think about the number of possible triangles each rotation makes. Look out for any patterns in the triangles for each rotation too.

Children should look at the shaded <u>and</u> non-shaded triangles when they're trying to spot patterns/shapes.

Section Three — Measurement and Geometry

Key Stage 2 Maths Investigations — Year 5

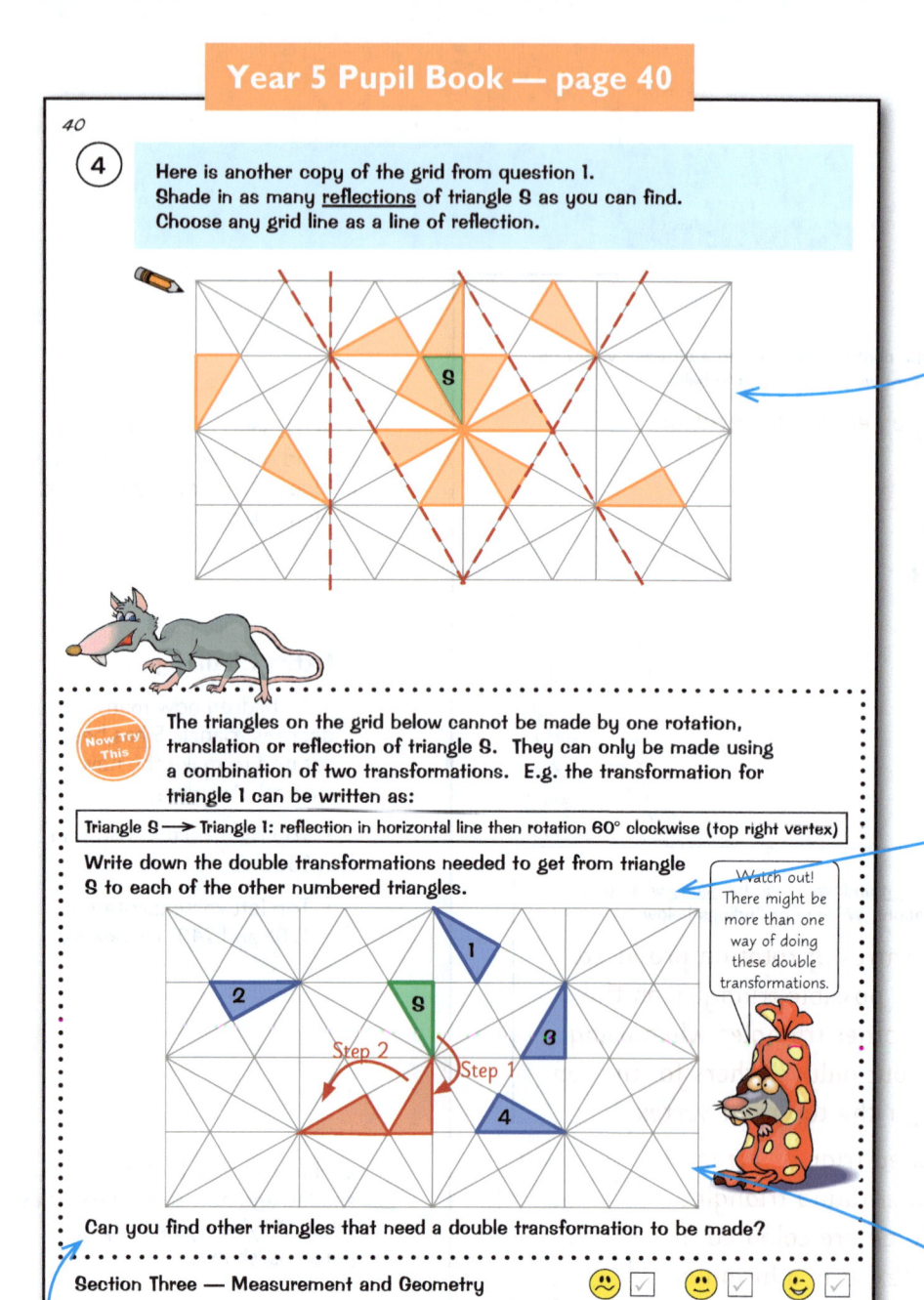

Triangle Transformations

Year 5 Pupil Book — page 40

④ Here is another copy of the grid from question 1.
Shade in as many <u>reflections</u> of triangle S as you can find.
Choose any grid line as a line of reflection.

Now Try This — The triangles on the grid below cannot be made by one rotation, translation or reflection of triangle S. They can only be made using a combination of two transformations. E.g. the transformation for triangle 1 can be written as:

Triangle S ⟶ Triangle 1: reflection in horizontal line then rotation 60° clockwise (top right vertex)

Write down the double transformations needed to get from triangle S to each of the other numbered triangles.

Watch out! There might be more than one way of doing these double transformations.

Can you find other triangles that need a double transformation to be made?

Section Three — Measurement and Geometry

- Children are likely to see reflections in vertical and horizontal lines first.
- Encourage them to turn the page around to see some of the other lines triangle S can be reflected in. The red dashed lines show the lines of reflection for some triangles that are further from the centre of the grid.

Triangle S ⟶ Triangle 2: rotation 60° clockwise (top left vertex) then reflection in vertical line

Triangle S ⟶ Triangle 3: rotation 120° clockwise (bottom vertex) then reflection in diagonal line (to the right)

Triangle S ⟶ Triangle 4: rotation 180° (bottom vertex) then rotation (bottom right vertex) 120° clockwise

There's only one example given for each of these double transformations, but there might be more than one way of doing each one.

Answers will vary. Children should perform two transformations on triangle S to locate new positions for triangles, such as the one shown above:

Step 1: reflection in horizontal line.

Step 2: rotation 120° anti-clockwise (bottom left vertex).

Showing Greater Depth

Children working at Greater Depth will be able to:
- (Q3 Show Your Thinking) analyse all of the images they have drawn and notice that different centres of rotation produce different numbers of triangles.

Key Stage 2 Maths Investigations — Year 5

Pulse Rate Line Graphs

Children need to know how to read line graphs, and should have had experience of drawing line graphs. They'll be reading data from a line graph and learning how to tell the story of a line of data. They'll generate their own data by recording their pulse rates after exercise and using them to draw line graphs with different axes, which they will look at to explore how the scales on a graph affect how it looks.

Aims:

- Solve comparison, sum and difference problems using information presented in a line graph.
- Collect and record data.
- Create a line graph.
- Consider how changing the scales on the axes affects the appearance of a line graph.

Key Vocabulary:
'line graph', 'y-axis', 'x-axis'

Resources Needed:
Ruler, space to exercise, stopwatch.

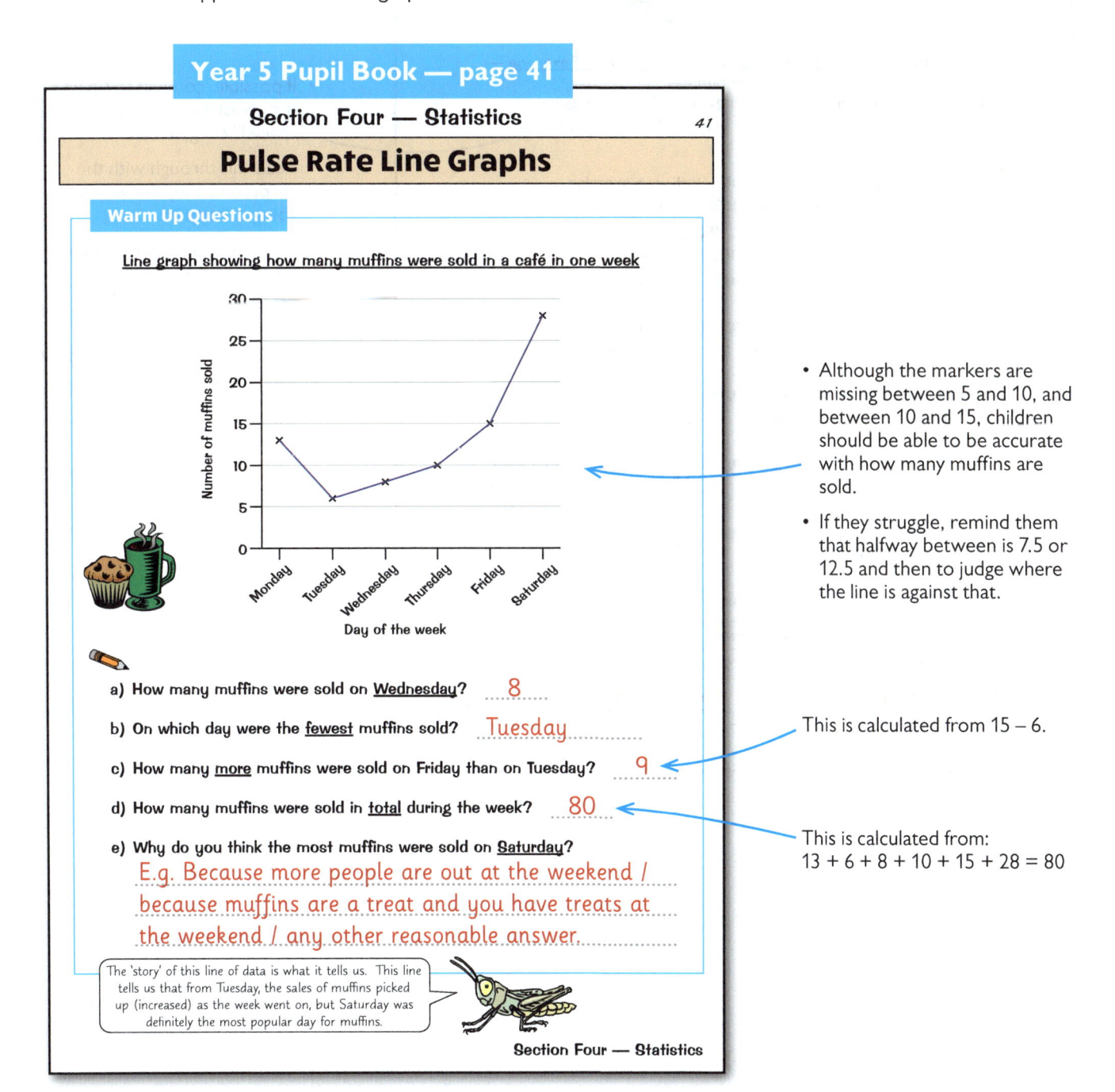

Year 5 Pupil Book — page 41

Section Four — Statistics

Pulse Rate Line Graphs

Warm Up Questions

Line graph showing how many muffins were sold in a café in one week

a) How many muffins were sold on Wednesday? **8**

b) On which day were the fewest muffins sold? **Tuesday**

c) How many more muffins were sold on Friday than on Tuesday? **9**

d) How many muffins were sold in total during the week? **80**

e) Why do you think the most muffins were sold on Saturday?
E.g. Because more people are out at the weekend / because muffins are a treat and you have treats at the weekend / any other reasonable answer.

The 'story' of this line of data is what it tells us. This line tells us that from Tuesday, the sales of muffins picked up (increased) as the week went on, but Saturday was definitely the most popular day for muffins.

- Although the markers are missing between 5 and 10, and between 10 and 15, children should be able to be accurate with how many muffins are sold.
- If they struggle, remind them that halfway between is 7.5 or 12.5 and then to judge where the line is against that.

This is calculated from 15 − 6.

This is calculated from:
13 + 6 + 8 + 10 + 15 + 28 = 80

Key Stage 2 Maths Investigations — Year 5

Pulse Rate Line Graphs

Pulse rates will vary but should be between 60 and 100 bpm.

Year 5 Pupil Book — page 42

① Take your pulse for 15 seconds and record your data below. Then calculate what this is in beats per minute.

E.g.
My pulse rate: 17 beats per 15 seconds
My pulse rate: 68 beats per minute (bpm)

We call your pulse rate your 'resting heart rate' when it is taken at a time of not doing very much.

Extra Support

Check before starting the activity that children know how to find their pulse. If a child is struggling to find their pulse, they can put their hand over their heart.

② In a moment (not yet!) you are going to do 1 minute of exercise — running on the spot, star jumps or burpees.
You're going to work really hard to get your heart rate going.
READ WHAT'S GOING TO HAPPEN below before you start.

E.g.
Exercise — When your teacher says GO, start your exercise.
When your teacher says STOP, sit down straight away.

0 min — When your teacher says GO, take your pulse for 15 seconds until they say STOP. Write it here: 40 beats per 15 seconds.

1 min — Your teacher will say GO again. Take your pulse until they say STOP. Write it here: 30 beats per 15 seconds.

2 min — Your teacher will say GO again. Take your pulse until they say STOP. Write it here: 23 beats per 15 seconds.

3 min — Your teacher will say GO again. Take your pulse until they say STOP. Write it here: 19 beats per 15 seconds.

4 min — Your teacher will say GO again. Take your pulse until they say STOP. Write it here: 18 beats per 15 seconds.

Now fill in the table by converting your pulse rates into beats per minute.

| Pulse rate (in bpm) taken ___ minutes after exercise |
0 min	1 min	2 min	3 min	4 min
160	120	92	76	72

Section Four — Statistics

- If possible, conduct this part of the investigation in a large space like a gym hall.
- Read this through with the children so they know what is going to happen.
- You will need to time 1 minute for the children to do their exercise. Make sure they then sit down immediately.
- As soon as they're settled, time the 15 seconds for the first pulse measurement. Keep the stopwatch running and start each subsequent pulse measurement at the start of each full minute.

Pulse Rate Line Graphs

Year 5 Pupil Book — page 43

③ Plot your data on each of these sets of axes.

A Line graph showing my pulse rate after exercise

B Line graph showing my pulse rate after exercise

C Line graph showing my pulse rate after exercise

Think about why the graphs have different shapes, even though they present the same data.

Section Four — Statistics

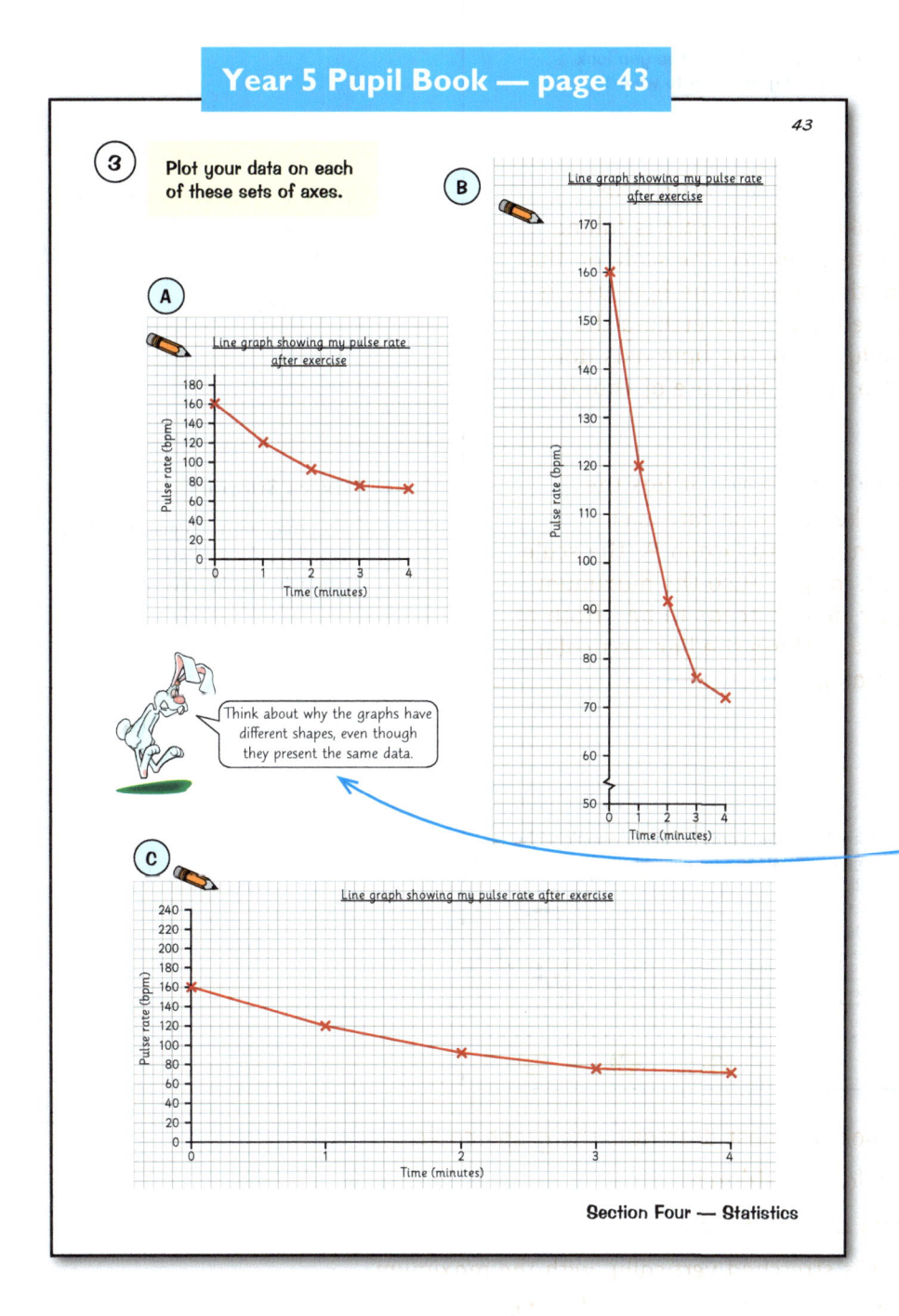

Extra Support
Advise children to plot each point carefully and then use a ruler to join the points with straight lines.

This is to get children thinking about how the scale of the axes has an impact on the way the plotted data looks. It'll come in handy for the next page.

Key Stage 2 Maths Investigations — Year 5

Pulse Rate Line Graphs

Year 5 Pupil Book — page 44

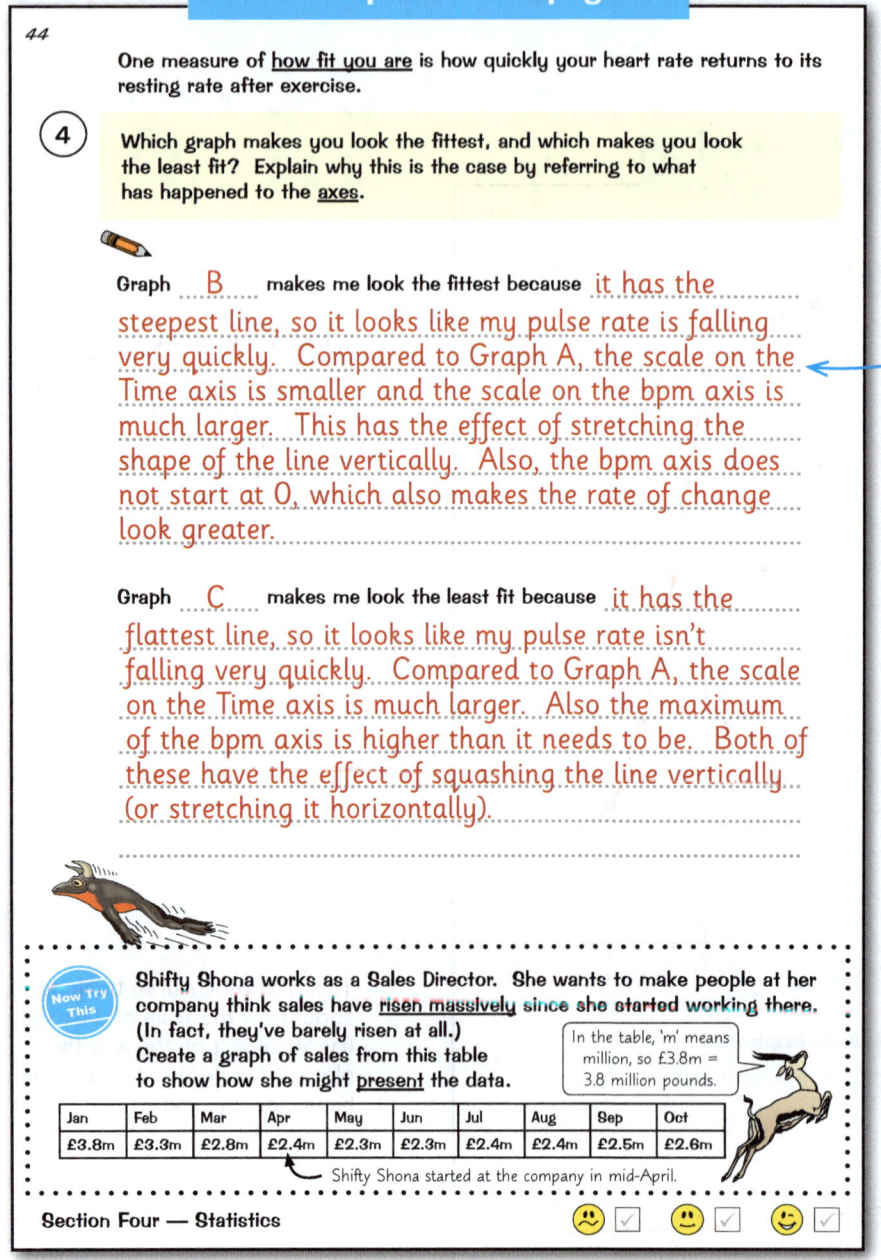

One measure of how fit you are is how quickly your heart rate returns to its resting rate after exercise.

4) Which graph makes you look the fittest, and which makes you look the least fit? Explain why this is the case by referring to what has happened to the axes.

Graph **B** makes me look the fittest because *it has the steepest line, so it looks like my pulse rate is falling very quickly. Compared to Graph A, the scale on the Time axis is smaller and the scale on the bpm axis is much larger. This has the effect of stretching the shape of the line vertically. Also, the bpm axis does not start at 0, which also makes the rate of change look greater.*

Graph **C** makes me look the least fit because *it has the flattest line, so it looks like my pulse rate isn't falling very quickly. Compared to Graph A, the scale on the Time axis is much larger. Also the maximum of the bpm axis is higher than it needs to be. Both of these have the effect of squashing the line vertically (or stretching it horizontally).*

When the y-axis doesn't start at 0, like Graph B, it's said to be 'truncated'. This has the effect of exaggerating the differences in data points.

Extra Support

You may want to give pupils a word bank, e.g. 'stretch', 'squash', 'scale', 'compared to'.

Now Try This — Shifty Shona works as a Sales Director. She wants to make people at her company think sales have risen massively since she started working there. (In fact, they've barely risen at all.) Create a graph of sales from this table to show how she might present the data.

In the table, 'm' means million, so £3.8m = 3.8 million pounds.

Jan	Feb	Mar	Apr	May	Jun	Jul	Aug	Sep	Oct
£3.8m	£3.3m	£2.8m	£2.4m	£2.3m	£2.3m	£2.4m	£2.4m	£2.5m	£2.6m

Shifty Shona started at the company in mid-April.

Section Four — Statistics

E.g. To make the rise in sales look the most dramatic, the graph could:
- miss out the data from January-March.
- have a y-axis that starts at, say, £2.2m.
- have a y-axis scale that is stretched vertically, with the maximum value on the y-axis close to the October value (£2.6m).

Showing Greater Depth

Children working at Greater Depth will be able to:
- (Now Try This) transfer their understanding of the concept of 'misleading graphs' so that they draw their own using the given data.

Key Stage 2 Maths Investigations — Year 5